T0064298

P.R.E.A.C.H

EMMANUEL KWAME BEMPONG

Trafford rev. 08/07/2014

 www.trafford.com

North America & international
toll-free: 1 888 232 4444 (USA & Canada)
fax: 812 355 4082

Contents

PREACH

Repentance
End times
Atonement
Confession
Holy Spirit

Man of God:
Emmanuel Kwame Bempong

PREACH

Repentance

End times

Atonement

Confession

Holy Spirit

He said to them *"Go into the entire world and* **preach** *the good news to all creation. Whoever believes and is baptized will be saved, but whoever does not believe will be condemned. And these signs will accompany those who believe. In my name they will drive out demons; they will speak in new tongues; they will pick up snakes with their hands and when they drink deadly poison, it will not hurt them at all; they will place their hands on sick people and they will get well.*

(Mark 16:15-18)

Dedication

I dedicate this book to all preachers, bishops, apostles, evangelists, prophets and prophetess, pastors, ministers, men and women of God all over the world.

Also to all followers of Jesus Christ, believers and unbelievers in fact every single soul that exist on this planet, May the lord use this divine insight and foresight to convict you on the wrong path, direct and guide your steps also help you escape from disaster.

Amen.

Acknowledgment

There is no way this book would have been published without giving reverence and a sacrificial thankfulness to God almighty.

Also to the special and wonderful people in my life that encouraged me to accomplish this task, may the lord reward you abundantly?

In addition I pray to the lord almighty to help me give thanks to Vida G. Lebene for being my help and support on this assignment may the lord also help you from his holy sanctuary and grant you support from mount Zion in all your endeavors.

FOREWORD

By fore-wording this book i have been sensitized with the dynamics, deeper, greater and higher knowledge of the Holy Spirit and the true purpose of Jesus Christ the son of our reigning God's mission assign to us on earth and as his disciples.

Therefore i urge any living soul reading this book should not reject the word but be injected by the word in to their spiritual and physical life to be able be perfect as our reigning God is perfect.

I currently know the author of the book as a member of my church, a humble and a visionary servant of God and i support him with the strength of God and heaven's embarkation in his endeavors and may the Lord continue to move him from grace to glory.

- Amen.

Founder/General overseer:
Reigning Power Gospel Church international
Rev. Dr. Samuel Sarpong Kwakwa

Summary

Preaching must always be rooted in biblical truth and dependent on the Holy Spirit; these elements are the foundational of preaching. And the following powerful verses rooted from the bible are what inspired the accomplishment of this book.

> He said to them *"Go into the entire world and **preach** the good news to all creation.*
>
> **-Mark 16:15**

> *"For **false Christ** and **prophets** will appear and perform great signs and miracles to deceive even the elect – if that were possible."*
>
> **-Matthew 24:24**

> *"For the **preaching** of the cross is the power of God".*
>
> **-1 Corinthians 1:18**

> *At this I fell at his feet to worship him. But he said to me do not do it! I am a fellow servant with you and with your brothers who hold to the testimony of Jesus. Worship God!* ***For the testimony of Jesus Christ is the spirit of Prophesy.***
>
> **-Revelation 19:10**

And in this book are the future prophecy about the *end times (technology)* – *a deeper insight of the mark of the beast (666)* and a powerful revelation about rapper kenye Omari West and the music industry.

Also the significance of the *Holy Spirit*; how necessary for every believer to be baptized in the *Holy Spirit*.

Again upon all the spiritual gifts of the *Holy Spirit* why is Jesus Christ so particular about the **Gift of Prophecy**; that getting to the end of the world *false Christ and prophets* shall rise up to deceive many even the elected ones of God?.

Sponsors

- E-Save Distributions and Investments.
- E-Save Travel and Tours Inc.
- E-Save Foundation (NGO)
- E-Save Real Estates
- E-Save Productions

INTRODUCTION

During my fourth time in London – United Kingdom, while praying and meditating on the deep revelation i was hearing through the voice of the Holy Spirit in my room, a Powerful word "**Preach**" touched my heart and suddenly it begun to tap into my thought.

I begun to wonder and felt deeply interested to understand the powerful word **preach** which has fell on my heart and has been accepted by my spirit to listen to the Holy Spirit, what He has to explain to me about this powerful and wonderful word.

Obediently I therefore asked myself why "*preach*" because I already know what is **preach** and I have been preaching in churches, to my friends and family, love ones even I have publish a book to promote the powerful elements of God and the Kingdom Business. Then what is so special and particular about the word **preach** again.

Apparently, the revelation about this word "*preach*" begun to manifest in my thought; to comprehend how this word is not just a common word but the word itself has its own meaning; it has something powerful in it. The word itself is a revelation to mankind, I therefore said to myself that I believe that to **preach**: -

- Is to proclaim or make known in a sermon.

- To deliver (the gospel).
- To advocate (moral principles, conduct) as right or advisable.

Therefore what would this word mean again apart from the above definition? Little did I know that there is powerful meanings in the word preach.

The Holy Spirit then asked me; have I consider trying to think of what the alphabets that sum up to form this word "*preach*" stands for? I said to myself no! I haven't.

Suddenly by the insight and revelation of the Holy Spirit it helped me to figure out what exactly this alphabets means to the word "**PREACH**".

The Holy Spirit asked me a question; what at all does Jesus Christ wants us to preach about when he ushers us to "**PREACH**" his word to the entire world.

> *"And He said to them, Go into the entire world and* **preach** *and publish openly the good news (The Gospel) to every creature [of the whole human race. He who believes [who adheres to, trusts in and relies on the Gospel and Him whom it sets forth] and is baptized will be saved [from the penalty of eternal death]; but he who does not and trust in and rely on the Gospel and Him whom it sets forth] will be condemned. And these attesting signs will ac-company those who believe: in my name will speak in new language; they will pick up serpent; and [even] if they drink anything deadly, it will not hurt them; they will lay their hand on the sick, and they will get well".*

(Mark 16:15-18)

I answered that; *his birth, death, the cross, resurrection and how by his blood we are all saved from the hands of the enemy (Satan). Therefore the devil doesn't have power over us anymore, because by his blood we are healed, blessed and rich.* We were made of perishable seed but by his blood through Christ Jesus we are now made of imperishable seed.

"For you have been born again, not of perishable seed, but of imperishable, through the living and enduring word of God."

(1 Peter 123)

The Holy Spirit asked me again, all I have answered is good but do I ask my self that after I have enjoyed and been blessed by what I preach to people, do God or does Jesus Christ benefit from the Sermon I have preached and do I make sure that the importance or the significance of the six alphabets that makes the word "PREACH" have been achieved?

I marveled and still soliloquizing (talking to my self), what achievement and what is there again after a wonderful sermon about the gospel being preached.

Gradually, the Holy Spirit tuned my attention and truly breaks the alphabets down and again tried to make me understand each and every single alphabet of the word "PREACH".

The Holy Spirit began to take me through this word "PREACH" alphabet by alphabet and by the divine power of God I was hit and deeply touched by the powerful revelation of the word "PREACH"; meaning: we should **Preach Repentance, End times** and also teach the people **Atonement** to help them **confess** their sins and be baptized in the **Holy Spirit.**

- Preach
- Repentance (Revelation)
- End time
- Atonement (procedure of forgiveness)
- Confession of Sin
- Holy Spirit Baptizm

Oh my God! My gracious God does that means all that I have known and preach to the world is of no benefit to you and your Kingdom. Infact I was marveled astonished but at the same time happy for a higher, greater and another deeper revelation from the Holy Spirit.

Precious one this is very powerful and I pray that no one can dispute the fact that the Holy Spirit is beyond genius. Overwhelmingly I bow my face to the floor to worship the Lord and begun to ask for forgiveness of preaching anything to the world which never benefited the kingdom of God.

Precious lord so as you said *"we shouldn't add or subtract anything apart from your word"* I have been ignorant of this till today, father God please forgive me and from today let me be a victim of these message and proclaim this greater, higher and deeper revelation to the four corners of the universe. I pray to you God that let me be a victim of the Cross and let the testimony of Jesus Christ rest upon my life.

CHAPTER ONE

PREACH

Precious one reading this book, It has been my desire to share this greater, higher and deeper revelation with you for you to also realize and analyzed it yourself, what's going on in the world today whether men and women of God or Christians are doing what we are supposed to do by Jesus Christ our lord and master savior when he ushers and urges us to go into all over the world to preach His message *"the gospel"* about the cross and his Kingdom.

> He said to them *"Go into the entire world and **preach** the good news to all creation. Whoever believes and is baptized will be saved, but whoever does not believe will be condemned. And these signs will accompany those who believe. In my name they will drive out demons; they will speak in new tongues; they will pick up snakes with their hands and when they drink deadly poison, it will not hurt them at all; they will place their hands on sick people and they will get well"*.

(Mark 16:15-18)

Beloved I never knew how the word *"preach"* is so important until the Holy Spirit divinely revealed the true meaning of this

1

word to me and I thank God that I have not been selfish by keeping this revelation to my self but have been able to be Obedient to stop all that I have been doing to listen and depend on what God wants me to know and also take my time to write them down and published it as a book.

I humbly say that it is not by my might or by my power but is the doing of the lord for this revelation to be born to you.

At this point, I believe we all know our lord and master savior Jesus Christ who was born to us by a virgin called *Mary* by the power of God and through the manifestation of the Holy Spirit. He grew in the body and form of mankind yet not of man decision, fulfilled his purpose on earth by *"preaching"* the word-gospel meaning repentance and the kingdom of God to his people.

*"From that time Jesus began to **preach**, "Repent for the kingdom of heaven is near"*

(Matthew 4:17)

Jesus Christ then died by being flogged and crucified on the cross and later in three days he resurrected from death and achieved the power and the greatest glory in the kingdom of his father by being placed at the right hand side of God.

Believers when Christ Jesus our lord and master savior was taken up into heaven, He said to his disciples present with him at that time to…

*"Go into the entire world and **preach** and publish openly the good news (The Gospel) to every creature [of the whole human race.*

Friends, the above scripture totally explain to us what Jesus Christ needs us to do in (verse 15). *"Go into all the world and **Preach** the good news to all creation".*

For we are not to doubt these revelation of the Holy Spirit, we can see it ourselves from the scriptures that yes indeed Christ Jesus need us to go and Preach this word to all creation all over the world.

And truly, from the day this was told to his disciples who were present with him at that time when he was taken up into heaven;

the message of Jesus Christ has traveled from time to time to our generation which I believe is all about promoting the good news of Christ Jesus and His kingdom.

But the revelation is that; are we preaching what we are supposed to preach or we are just preaching because Jesus Christ wanted us to preach. Children of God this is very deep and my thought has been itching for a deeper, higher and greater revelation, I continue to ask myself "*like what at all are we really missing here?* The Holy Spirit ministered unto me, yes of course we are preaching but some of the messages we are preaching are being corrupted by worldly gains and frictions that we called *prophesy* to corrupt the mind of the people. This is a perfect reason why God sent his prophet Jeremiah to his people concerning the prophets and the priests.

> "*Concerning the prophets: my heart is broken within me; all my bones tremble. I am like a drunken man like a man overcome by wine because of the lord and his holy words.*
>
> *The land is full of adulterers because of the curse the land lies parched and the pastures in the desert are withered. The prophets follow an evil course and use their power unjustly.*
>
> *Both prophets and priest are godless; even in my temple I find their wickedness, declares the lord. Therefore their path will become slippery they will be banished to darkness and there they will fall. I will bring disaster on them in the year they are punished, declares the lord.*
>
> *Among the prophets of Samaria I saw this repulsive thing: they prophesied by Baal and led my people Israel astray. Among the prophets of Jerusalem I have seen Something horrible. They commit adultery and live a lie. They strengthen the hands of evil doers so that no one turns from his wickedness. They are all like Sodom to me the people of Jerusalem are like Gomorrah. Therefore this is what the Lord almighty says concerning the prophets: I will make them eat bitter food and drink poisoned water*

because from the prophets of Jerusalem ungodliness has spread throughout the land.

This is what the Almighty says: **do not listen to what the Prophets are prophesying to you; they fill you with false hopes. They speak visions from their own minds not from the mouth of the lord.**

They keep saying to those who despise me, the lord says: you will have peace. And to all the stubbornness of their hearts they say, No harm will come to you. But which of them has stood in the council of the Lord to see or to hear his word? Who has listened and heard his word?

See the storm of the Lord will burst out in wrath, a whirlwind swirling down on the heads of the wicked. The anger of the Lord will not turn back until he fully accomplishes the purposes of his heart. In days to come you will understand it clearly.

I did not send these prophets yet they have run with their message I did not speak to them yet they have prophesied. *But if they had stood in my council, they would have proclaimed my words to my people and would have turned them from their evil ways and from their evil deeds.*

Am I only a God nearby, declares the Lord, and not a God far away? Can anyone hide in secret places so that I cannot see him declares the Lord. Do not I fill heaven and earth? Declares the Lord.

I have heard what the prophets say who prophesy lies in my name. They say I had a dream! I had a dream! How long will this continue in the hearts of these lying prophets, who prophesy the delusions of their own minds? *They think the dreams they tell one another will make my people forget my name, just as their fathers forgot my name through Baal worship.*

Let the prophet who has a dream tell his dream, but let the one who has my words speak it faithfully. For what

4

has straw to do with grain? Declares the Lord. Is it not my word like a hammer that breaks a rock into pieces?

Therefore declares the Lord, **I am against the prophets who steal from one another words supposedly from me.** *Yes, declares the Lord, I am against the Prophets who wag their own tongues and yet declare, the lord declares; in deed I am against those who prophesy false dreams, declares the lord. They tell them and led my people astray with their reckless lies, yet I did not send or appoint them. They do not benefit these people in the least, declares the Lord".*

(Jeremiah 23:9-32)

I truly thank the Holy Spirit for the above scripture which is true because many preachers have diversify the message from the realities of the cross of Jesus Christ and about his kingdom to preach prosperity, worldly gains, life anxieties, riches and success whilst they have refused to **Preach, Repentance** (revelation) **End times** for the people to gain **Atonement** and **Confess** their sins to receive the **Holy Spirit** Baptizm.

So this is the meaning of the word **PREACH -:**

Preaching, Repentance, End time, Atonement, Confession and Holy Spirit Baptizm.

This is exactly what it means to *"preach"* confirmed and affirmed by the Holy Spirit.

Preach   - Good News
Repentance   - sorrow of sin and turning to God.
End time   - MARK of the Beast-666/ Technology/ Music-Entertainment.
Atonement   - Procedure of forgiveness and sacrifices.
Confession   - Confessing our sins
Holy Spirit Baptizm - Advocate, guidance help us walk in holiness.

Therefore my brothers and sisters the above words and meaning is what Jesus Christ meant when he sent us to go and *preach* the gospel to the entire world and I declare to you that from day one till today the heartbeat of God Is for us to *preach* his word to the world.

I believe you are beginning to put yourself in my shoes now and I pray for you to feel how I felt when I first understood the word "**PREACH**".

Beloved this truly makes sense and I am in love with the Holy Spirit for such a gift of understanding and revelation.

Infact looking around my self, the environment, society, the community and what is being preached in the world today through the media, in churches, television, radio and at times conferences and mega fest which are being organized by many preachers; has deviated from the word **preach** which the lord has commanded us to do as his children and disciples.

Today millions of churches and preacher's are preaching only prosperity, how to gain wealth, how to be successful in our business and others, by making the congregation donate and sowing consecrated and prophetic seeds for them to live in big mansions, buy houses all over the world, driving and riding in luxurious cars and wearing the best quality of cloths ever.

> But the bible even declares that *"But if we have food and clothing we will be content with that, people who want to get rich fall into temptation and a trap and into many foolish and harmful desires that plunge men into ruin and destructions, for the love of money is a root of all kinds of evil. Some people eager for money have wandered from the faith and pierced themselves with many grief's."*
>
> (1 Timothy 6:8-10)

Yes! I believe that we as children of God need to be rich and successful but have we consider by telling them and explaining to the ignorant congregation that after gaining all this wealth and we die, we are not going to take nothing with us, and we will still leave everything we have labored for here in God's universe.

> *"For we brought nothing into the world and we can take nothing out of it."*
>
> (1 Timothy 6:7)

Have we preachers taken our time to let them know of what benefit will it be after gaining all the riches, success, property, luxury and anything we could think of, some righteously and others unrighteous; we will not even take just a penny with us on the day we die and leave this earth.

May be some preachers have been doing it may be some other preachers are not doing it.

However, are we achieving our goals, are we making Jesus Christ and his kingdom benefit from what we have been preaching.

By preaching; do we achieve the deeper, greater and higher revelation or insight in the word *"preach"*.

Beloved, this is very deep and I want you to humbly accept the revelation by faith and from today begin to preach what is needed to be preached by **preaching** about Repentance (revelation), **End time** to the church for them to gain the insight of **Atonement** and **confess** their sins to receive the Baptizm of the **Holy Spirit**.

Men and Women of God this is what Jesus Christ wants us to Preach for his kingdom to benefit, thus why he has called and chosen us to do his work. He has trusted us that we can do it and has given us gift and power to use it to operate and draw souls, bring back the captive from the camp of hell to his kingdom.

But in today's churches, is all about operating in the gifts of God to gain wealth and live luxurious lives. This is why the bible declares that;

> *"If anyone teaches false doctrines and does not agree to the sound instruction of our lord Jesus Christ and to godly teaching. He is conceited and understands nothing. He has an unhealthy interest in controversies and quarrels about words that result in envy, strife, malicious talk, evil suspicions and constant friction between men of corrupt mind, who have been robbed of the truth and who think that godliness is a means to financial gain".*

(1 Timothy 6:3-5)

God is not saying we shouldn't live good lives or have luxury moments but our focus shouldn't be that of gaining riches alone because based on that the devil have come to sit on our minds and also sat on so many churches, he has provide many men and women of God with much money to blind them from speaking what is truth to the church.

Many believers have forgotten about the cross of Jesus Christ and have even forget that he will come again because we are busy preaching what is going to make us rich and wealthier but have we also forgotten that later we are going to perish.

From my experienced I have seen the gospel of God progressive, through the television, radio, magazines, newspapers, the media etc. Big time conferences and mega fest are being held in different parts of the world, I think the word of God is almost everywhere now and forcefully getting to the four corners of the world.

But of what benefit will it be to Jesus Christ and His Kingdom though we are preaching but specifically not preaching what he really needed us to *preach*.

In our world today, if you are not a prophet or can't prophecy you are not qualified as a true man of God, because every body and anyone is prophesying. If you can't prophecy you can not even be invited to preach in peoples churches.

But I tell you the truth we have miss the true word of God, the good news of Christ Jesus and have focus on trying to study and learning how to prophecy to please the church and the congregation and also wants to gain favour in the sight of the world.

Men and women of God today are prophesying to make and gain luxury from their congregation, allowing them to bring prophetic, consecrated and divine seeds of money for the prophetic word to be released on them.

Yes! Of course, this is what is happening in the world of today; if you are not a prophet you don't gain favor from your church or your fellow preachers.

And this has let many true men and women of God lost their way to eternal destruction.

"My people from lack of knowledge my people perish".

(Hosea 4:6)

Precious one, prophecy is good but prophecy shouldn't be a competition between churches, it shouldn't bring diversity in the church, it shouldn't bring jealousy in the church. But rather encourage the people in the church said by Apostle Paul in the book of...

(1 Corinthians 14:3)

But everyone who prophesies speaks to men for their strengthening, encouragement and comfort.

Infact the Bible declares that getting to the Endtime of this world there will be false prophets and false Christ's to deceive people yet people have allowed themselves to be deceived because of life anxieties, gaining wealth, riches and trying to live luxury lives through the prophetic word given to them by various prophets.

But the bible convicts us to be alert of false Christ and prophets during this time in the world.

"For false Christ and prophets will appear and perform great signs and miracles to deceive even the elect – if that were possible."

(Matthew 24:24)

I believe the *End time* is already here thus why people fancy prophecy now a day as if prophecy is fashion.

But we should not be ignorant that some of these prophecy and prophets or prophetesses are not from God. This is why the bible declares in Jeremiah the prophet:

"I did not send these Prophets yet they have run with their message; I did not speak to them yet they have prophesied."

(Jeremiah 23:21)

9

People of God, prophetic Mantle is a gift from God which if the lord does not chose you as his prophet we shouldn't go to other prophets to study, learn and practice how to prophecy.

Yes! Believers if you are not aware many people are learning how to prophecy to gain fame and wealth because of how the prophetic gift has greater influence in the church or in the world today.

"Therefore declares the Lord; I am against the prophets who steal from one another words supposedly from me"

(Jeremiah 23:30)

Even my self have been a victim of this situation but glory be to God that, I didn't fall for the influence of this learning of how to prophecy.

These happened when a nice young prophet friend of mine whom I visited his church during one of his prophetic programs. In fact how he prophesy was very marvelous, it was very interesting how he was operating in the prophetic gift.

He mentioned the first and last names of some people, their phone numbers, things that has already happen in their family, their house addresses even down to their bank account numbers.

In fact this was very powerful, wonderful and very attractive and believe me, it was surprising to everyone at the church.

People of God this gift is very Powerful and if you ask me I will tell you that the prophetic gift really attract souls both believers and unbelievers which is very good because at the end of the day souls are been drawn to God.

But one thing we must understand is; drawing someone closer to someone is different from making someone truly know and accept whom he or she is drawing closer to.

Because many people might dance to the music because of its rhythm and because the music sounds good (entertainment) but what about if the music stopped playing and it doesn't feel or look like entertainment any more, are the people going to endure the circumstances or fall back. These means we should let the church know that the kingdom of God is not all about prophetic and prophecies.

> This is why the bible declares that *;" let the prophet who has a dream tell his dream but let the one who has my word speak it faithfully. For what has straw to do with grain." Declares the Lord "*

(Jeremiah 23:28)

Believers, after that program of my friend at his church we went to sat in his office and I was telling him how beautiful and supernatural gift he has and was operating, trust me it looks very attractive and am very much in love with such a gift.

But he turned to me and said to me that they are prophetic keys which if I am cool or okay with it he is going to teach me, "wow"! I said to myself in my mind *"prophetic keys"* then I believe is great and I can't wait to be given these key or know of these keys.

But people of God when the Holy Spirit took me deeper and revealed the unsearchable things to me I understood from the scripture that the prophetic gift is a gift from God but not a gift from mankind to mankind and even if it will be from mankind to mankind it should be authorized by God.

But I asked myself, what if these keys get missing or get lost or does God want me to be his prophet or he wants me to operate in a different gift therefore If I forced myself to be given a prophetic key from my fellow man, I am limiting my self to the dream, visions, ideas and spiritual gift God himself have installed in me or for me.

> Besides I also remember from the Holy Scriptures that *"A man does nothing until he has been authorized from heaven above".*

(John 3: 27)

> And *"the lord also gives the spirit or the gift without limit".*

(John 3:34).

Believes, God have promised us that *"ears have not heard and eyes have not seen what the almighty God have installed for us his children".*

(1 Corinthians 2:9).

Therefore if some one should be a prophet another man should be an evangelist, pastor, Apostles, bishops or something else. But because the gift of prophecy is interesting, entertaining, encouraging and attractive everyone in the world today wants to be or wants to turn into a prophet.

But we the sons and daughters of the most High God should be more vigilant and read the Holy Scriptures more to enlighten ourselves for us not to be deceived by false prophets and their false, planned and arranged prophecies.

For the bible even declares that they speak this from their own minds "how *long will this continue in the hearts of these lying prophets, who prophesy the delusions of their own minds"*

(Jeremiah 23:26)

Let me tell you a powerful story from the Holy Spirit about a man called Saul who was later named Paul from the book of...

(Acts 16:16-19).

"Once when we were going to the place of prayer, we were met by a female slave who had a spirit by which she predicted the future. She earned a great deal of money for her owners by fortune-telling. 17 She followed Paul and the rest of us, shouting, "These men are servants of the Most High God, who are telling you the way to be saved." 18 She kept this up for many days. Finally Paul became so annoyed that he turned around and said to the spirit, "In the name of Jesus Christ I command you to come out of her!" At that moment the spirit left her.19 When her owners realized that their hope of making money was gone, they seized Paul and Silas and dragged them into the marketplace to face the authorities".

12

Precious one, we realized from the above scripture that, Paul was a true man and a prophet of God who was preaching and miraculously signs and wonders where following.

But a demon possessed woman whom I will say she will be or has disguise herself as a prophetess tried to gain fame, get the people's attention and also wants to win the Christian market followed Paul and was prophecing good things about Paul. Believers, see how the devil can perform in the gift of prophecy and all that comes with it, this demonic possessed woman was proclaiming about Apostle Paul being a good prophet but her gift wasn't from God.

This is because she has realized that Paul was getting more fame, attention and winning souls for Christ Jesus, so she developed a plan and a very tricky plan of course to make people believe she is also a prophetess and all the gorgeous demonic work she has been performing is from God.

But Apostle Paul turned to the woman and rebuked the woman because he realized that the woman is demonic and all that she is doing is not from God but rather to gain fame, attention and win souls for his master Lucifer (Satan).

Jesus Christ of Nazareth! so we should just imagine that if Apostle Paul wasn't a true servant of God he was totally going to fall for what the demonic woman was doing but glory is to God that Apostle Paul realized and can identify the true Spirit of his master Jesus that he serves.

This tells me that Apostle Paul has the Spirit of discernment and ascendment to test that Spirit of the demonic woman. That is why the bible teaches us that we should test all Spirit and find the true spirit which is divinely sent from God almighty him self.

> *"Dear friends, do not believe everyone who claims to speak by the Spirit. You must test them to see if the spirit they have comes from God. **For there are many false prophets in the world**".*
>
> (1John 4:1)

13

Believers I want you to pray at this point for the gift of discernment and ascendment to test spirits that are from God and which are not from God for us not to be deceived by false and satanic prophets.

You might say that you are ignorant but that is why you have the Bible to learn day in day out to get to know God, Jesus Christ and the Holy Spirit.

Precious One, am not Saying Prophecy is not good or don't accept prophetic words or I am against the prophetic gift of God on peoples life. But is because at the end God is going to be the Judge of us all and I declare to you that look for God your self, Search and find God yourself knock and God will open all you need to you.

> *"Ask and it will be given to you; seek and you will find; knock and the door will be opened to you. For every one who asks receives; he who seeks finds; and to him who knocks, the door will be opened to him".*

(Matthew 7:7-8)

Brother and sisters, prophecy is good and it's the most essential and extraordinary gift from God, very sensitive, detailed and very pleasing and attracted to the soul of mankind.

That is why the Bible warns us that we should be very careful of such gift because during the *endtime* many false prophets will appear to deceive people, which means people are going to turn their selves prophets, some will visit sorcery to become prophets, others will learn, study and imitate others all in the name of gaining fame, wealth and wining the Christian market to snatch souls for Satan. But may the grace of our Lord Jesus Christ have mercy on us for our souls to be kept spotless and blameless for his second coming.

> But the bible even declares that: *"indeed, I am against those who prophesy false dreams, declares the Lord, they tell them and lead my people astray with their reckless lies, yet I did not send or appoint them"*

(Jeremiah 23:32)

Prophecy started from the beginning of the universe which is from the Old Testament to the New Testament God have been making, choosing and sending prophets to speak and deliver his messages. Prophecy is the massage from God through the manifestation of the Holy Spirit for mankind to speak what God have for his people in the future which is to direct and guide us for our destiny to be accomplished in the truth way, path or direction. Believers Jesus promised us of the Holy Spirit that, he will come to be our comforter, advocate and guidance.

"He is our helper, intercessor, advocate, strengthener and standby".

(John 14:13-21)

Now the bible also makes us understand the works of the Holy Spirit in the book of...

(John 16:5 – 16)

"But now I am going to Him Who sent me, yet none of you asks Me, Where are you going? ⁶But because I have said these things to you, sorrow has filled your hearts [taken complete possession of them (good, expedient, advantageous) for you that I go away. Because if I do not go away, the Comforter (Counselor, Helper, Advocate, Intercessor, Strengthener, Standby) will not come to you [into close fellowship with you]; but if I go away, I will send Him to you [to be in close fellowship with you]. ⁸And when He comes, He will convict and convince the world and bring demonstration to it about sin and about righteousness (uprightness of heart and right standing with God) and about judgment: ⁹About sin, because they do not believe in Me [trust in, rely on, and adhere to Me]; ¹⁰About righteousness (uprightness of heart and right standing with God), because I go to My Father, and you will see Me no longer; ¹¹About judgment, because the ruler (evil genius, prince) of this world [Satan] is judged and condemned and sentence already is passed upon him. ¹²I have still many things to say to you, but you are not able to bear them or to take them upon you

or to grasp them now.[13] *but when He, the Spirit of Truth (the Truth – giving Spirit) comes, He will guide you into all the Truth (the whole, full Truth). For He will not speak His own message [on His own authority]: but He will tell whatever He hears [from the Father; He will give the message that has been given to Him], and He will announce and declare to you the things that are to come [what will happen in the future].* [14]*He will honor and glorify Me, because He will take of (receive, draw upon) what is Mine and will reveal (declare, disclose, transmit) it to you.* [15]*Everything that the Father has is Mine, That is what I meant when I said that He [the Spirit] will take the things that are Mine and will reveal (declare, disclose, transmit) it to you.* [16]*In a little while you will no longer see me, and again after a short while you will see me".*

Children of God in the above scripture we found out that Jesus Christ is calling the Holy Spirit the Spirit of truth and the Spirit of truth will not speak on his own but He will speak only what He hears and he is going to tell us what is yet to come.

In fact I tell you sons and daughters of Christ Jesus the bible is good to read and the Holy Spirit will reveal the deep revelation of the Bible to you. Now we even realized that the Holy Spirit is not going to speak or prophecy on his own but what he hears from God. So that means if he doesn't hear anything he will not prophecy anything and if he should prophecy he will speak what is to come in the future and not what is behind us or past.

But many prophets of today prophecy about what is behind people the past of people which I believe has nothing to do with future as the bible says the Spirit will tell us what is yet to come that means is the future that will be proclaimed to us.

Beloved this totally explain to us what we need to know and be aware of true prophets and their prophecies whether is from God or not.

Now the scripture declares that we should let our *"Yes be our Yes and No be No; anything beyond this comes from the evil one."*

(Matthew 5:37)

So based on the above verse, why won't God himself let his Yes be his Yes and No be his No. Therefore for God to tell us that the Holy Spirit is going to tell us the truth of what he hears from God and the future things, which means there is no time for the Holy Spirit to go against God and be telling people or us our past things. People of God we should be much focus on how the prophets are prophesying in the world today. Some prophets can spend time to mention your first and last names, telephone numbers, the sins and curses of your fore fathers and even your bank account numbers.

Please people of God, this is very good and it's very powerful to do all this but of what benefit has it got to do with the things of the future because God is telling us that the Holy Spirit will tell us what is to come – that means *future*.

When God should speak to you or on your life by a prophet or through a prophet definably it shall come to pass because the word of God is powerful and is the power of God which removes burdens and break yokes of curses in our lives automatically;

> "*Is not my word like fire, declares the Lord and like a hammer that breaks a rock in pieces*"

(Jeremiah 23:29)

Therefore it doesn't matter about our telephone numbers, bank accounts numbers and our past sins, so far as God have spoken; everything God wants us to be and wants us to become it shall come to pass in his own perfect time.

Believer I am not saying prophecy is not good Prophecy is good but too much of emphasizing on the entertainment part of it makes us blind of dealing with repentance, the end time, accepting atonement and confessing our sine to receive the Holy Spirit and it Baptizm to be able to walk in Holiness.

Please if you will or can bear with me what has bank accounts numbers and telephone numbers got to do with the message of God. Please do we have to accept that without God proving to us by telling our bank account numbers and telephone numbers? He can't perform what he wants to perform in our lives?

Beloved God is the creator of the universe therefore he does not need the assurance of you believing or not what he wants to do in our live in the future. He is powerful, powerful than heaven and earth, he does thing without consulting any body.

> *"Can anyone hi de in secret places so that I cannot see him declares the Lord. Do not I fill heaven and earth declares the Lord. I have heard what the prophets say who prophesy lies in my name. They say I had a dream! I had a dream!"*

(Jeremiah 23:24-25)

Because of prophecy we have forgotten that God is a secret God therefore respect the privacy of mankind He doesn't tell things that will not or never benefit his kingdom. I know one will say prophesying - of saying people's accounts numbers, car and phone numbers is to make people believe God more.

But I tell you the truth the *blood* of Jesus Christ shared on the cross is greater, higher and a very powerful evidence for anyone and everyone who doesn't believe God should believe Him. Therefore he is coming again bringing to us what our sins, wicked acts and unrighteousness deserve.

> *"Behold I am coming soon! My reward is with me, and I will give to everyone according to what he has done."*

(Revelation 22:12)

Believers, God is telling us to **preach, repentance** (revelation), **end time** for people to accept **atonement** which is the procedure of forgiveness and **confess** their sins after that we should pray for them to know the **Holy Spirit** and it baptism to be able to live a righteous life.

But People are deceiving people with prophecy and prophetic conferences all over the world and this have blind us from the true good news of God.

And the bible gives us a clear warning that we shouldn't listen to them in the book of Jeremiah;

> *"This is what the Lord almighty says: do not listen to what the prophets are prophesying to you, they will fill you with*

false hopes. They speak visions from their own minds, not from the mouth of the Lord".

(Jeremiah 23:16)

You know before people used to go to the - medium's - fetish priest's - medicinal men - herbalist' (*malam's* - *agbala*) to look or see into their future and to know what's ahead of them also for protection and riches but now the rate of Christianity is very high so the devil has turn himself a prophet and has come to sit in the church and has capitalized on the prophetic ministry and still looking into people's future, prophesying and though he is prophesying what you believe is true to you; trust me the impartation and the end results will be very demonic.

People of God will you agree with me that the prophetic ministry is winning the Christian market; yes! Is good to prophesy but be careful as individuals whom you allow to prophesy to you or upon you. Prophesy can or will direct you but some prophesies can lead you into your destruction.

For devil (*prophet*) came to steal (*prophesy*) - kill (*demonic directions*) and destroy (*destruction-death*).

Devil — False Christ and false prophets.

Steal — False prophesies, teachings and delusions also rob you from knowing the truth.

Kill — Demonic directions and rob you of your money, riches and wealth.

Destroy — destructions, struggles, oppress you and it will lead you to your death.

Precious people I am not speaking against prophecy and prophets in the world but we must be aware of the true one's and what the Bible tells us about false prophets when it's getting to the end times of this world.

God did not said that there is going to be false evangelist, revivalist, pastors, apostles etc. But he rather mentioned a particular gift and it's title, this should tell us the truth because every one wants to be a prophet today whether is from God or not. Because that is where they can falsely say invalid things to you to make money out of you and live luxurious lives.

Believers we should read the Bible and we should know and understand what is needed from a prophet or of a prophet who is or has been sent from God.

For me, with my best of knowledge and the deeper revelation or insight of the holy spirit has let me know or revealed to me; I have realized that God is good and he does not listen to the prophets of the enemy (Satan) but rather listen and answers the prophets sent from Him.

Biblically, I had a revelation of Jesus Christ turning water into wine but he refused to turn stone in to bread. Hope we can remember this story from the Holy Scriptures;

> *"On the third day a wedding took place at Cana in Galilee. Jesus' mother was there, ² and Jesus and his disciples had also been invited to the wedding. ³ When the wine was gone, Jesus' mother said to him, "They have no more wine."*
>
> *⁴ "Woman,[a] why do you involve me?" Jesus replied. "My hour has not yet come."*
>
> *⁵ His mother said to the servants, "Do whatever he tells you."*
>
> *⁶ Nearby stood six stone water jars, the kind used by the Jews for ceremonial washing, each holding from twenty to thirty gallons.[b]*
>
> *⁷ Jesus said to the servants "Fill the jars with water"; so they filled them to the brim.⁸ then he told them, "Now draw some out and take it to the master of the banquet. "They did so, ⁹ and the master of the banquet tasted the water that had been turned into wine. He did not realize where it had come from, though the servants who had drawn the water knew. Then he called the bridegroom aside ¹⁰ and said, "Everyone brings out the choice wine first and then the cheaper wine after the guests have had too much to drink; but you have saved the best till now."*

[11] What Jesus did here in Cana of Galilee was the first of the signs through which he revealed his glory; and his disciples believed in him".

(John 2:1-11)

"Jesus, full of the Holy Spirit, left the Jordan and was led by the Spirit into the wilderness, 2 where for forty days he was tempted[a] by the devil. He ate nothing during those days, and at the end of them he was hungry. The devil said to him, "If you are the Son of God, tell this stone to become bread." Jesus answered, "It is written: 'Man shall not live on bread alone".

(Luke 4:1-4)

Beloved why is it that Jesus Christ from the scripture above changed water into wine but He didn't change the stone into bread. Please is it because the voice that told him to help, because they needed some wine is from a good source but the voice that told Jesus Christ to change the stone into bread wasn't from a good source or was it because he couldn't change the stone into bread.

But I declare to you that he could do it and even more than that, he would have change the stone into very expensive and rich bread but he realized that it wasn't from God.

Precious one this revelation also speaks to us that is not every prophet that speaks from God or have been authorized by God, That is why upon all the prophecies you have received from all the prophetic conference and services you have been to; you still struggle in your life, you continue to face bitterness in your life but day in day out they continue to prophecy upon your life but little do you know or did you know that those prophets have not been sent by God or have not been authorized by God.

You know lets take another picture from the Old Testament about Baal prophets and Prophet Elijah.

"So Ahab sent word throughout all Israel and assembled the prophets on Mount Carmel. [21] Elijah went before the people and said, "How long will you waver between two opinions? If the Lord is God, follow him; but if Baal is

God, follow him. "But the people said nothing.²² Then Elijah said to them, "I am the only one of the Lord's prophets left, but Baal has four hundred and fifty prophets. ²³ Get two bulls for us. Let Baal's prophets choose one for them, and let them cut it into pieces and put it on the wood but not set fire to it. I will prepare the other bull and put it on the wood but not set fire to it. ²⁴ Then you call on the name of your god, and I will call on the name of the Lord. The god who answers by fire—he is God."

Then all the people said, "What you say is good."

²⁵ Elijah said to the prophets of Baal "Choose one of the bulls and prepare it first, since there are so many of you. Call on the name of your god, but do not light the fire." ²⁶ So they took the bull given them and prepared it.

Then they called on the name of Baal from morning till noon. "Baal, answer us!" they shouted. But there was no response; no one answered. And they danced around the altar they had made.

²⁷ At noon Elijah began to taunt them. "Shout louder!" he said. "Surely he is a god! Perhaps he is deep in thought, or busy, or traveling. Maybe he is sleeping and must be awakened." ²⁸ So they shouted louder and slashed themselves with swords and spears, as was their custom, until their blood flowed. ²⁹ Midday passed, and they continued their frantic prophesying until the time for the evening sacrifice. But there was no response, no one answered, no one paid attention. ³⁰ Then Elijah said to all the people, "Come here to me." They came to him, and he repaired the altar of the Lord, which had been torn down. ³¹ Elijah took twelve stones, one for each of the tribes descended from Jacob, to whom the word of the Lord had come, saying, "Your name shall be Israel." ³² With the stones he built an altar in the name of the Lord, and he dug a trench around it large enough to hold two seahs[a] of seed. ³³ He arranged the wood, cut the bull into pieces and laid it on the wood. Then he said to them, "Fill four large jars with water and pour it on the offering and on the wood."

³⁴ "Do it again," he said, and they did it again.

"Do it a third time," he ordered, and they did it the third time. ³⁵ The water ran down around the altar and even filled the trench.

³⁶ At the time of sacrifice, the prophet Elijah stepped forward and prayed: "Lord, the God of Abraham, Isaac and Israel, let it be known today that you are God in Israel and that I am your servant and have done all these things at your command. ³⁷ Answer me, Lord, answer me, so these people will know that you, Lord, are God, and that you are turning their hearts back again."

³⁸ Then the fire of the Lord fell and burned up the sacrifice, the wood, the stones and the soil, and also licked up the water in the trench.

³⁹ When all the people saw this, they fell prostrate and cried, "The Lord—he is God! The Lord—he is God!"

⁴⁰ Then Elijah commanded them, "Seize the prophets of Baal. Don't let anyone get away!" They seized them, and Elijah had them brought down to the Kishon Valley and slaughtered there".

(1 kings 18:20-40)

Precious one would you just bear with me that the voice of Baal prophets wasn't heard and at the end of the day it brought them destruction but the voice of Elijah was heard and his request was fulfilled.

People of God I declare to you that if the one prophesying on your life is not from God or have not been authorized by God you will receive bundles of prophecies and yet it will bring you destructions instead of directions to retrieve your blessings.

I want you to continue to pray for God to give you more of his insight and foresight about false prophets in this end times, please if you can agree with me; in today's world we have too many prophets everybody is trying to be a prophet. I need you to ask yourself why it is so or that?

I will say because the *end time* is already here, so we should be very vigilant and cautious of their deceiving ways. They will tell you your home address, bank account numbers, first and last names, the directions to your house your date of birth and your past things.

Please God is doing and can do all this but I am asking you, of what benefit will God get or gain if He allow a prophet to tell you all this things, Plus how is this dates and numbers going to benefit the kingdom of God.

Precious one am not saying this is not real but I tell you that the devil (Satan) can also let someone do the same thing for you to consider him or her as a true prophet. Please I want us to remember the time of Moses when he was sent to Egypt to claim the Israelites from the hands of Pharaoh…

(Exodus 7:8-24).

The Lord said to Moses and Aaron, ⁹ "When Pharaoh says to you, 'Perform a miracle,' then say to Aaron, 'Take your staff and throw it down before Pharaoh,' and it will become a snake."

¹⁰ So Moses and Aaron went to Pharaoh and did just as the Lord commanded. Aaron threw his staff down in front of Pharaoh and his officials, and it became a snake. ¹¹ Pharaoh then summoned wise men and sorcerers, and the Egyptian magicians also did the same things by their secret arts: ¹² Each one threw down his staff and it became a snake. But Aaron's staff swallowed up their staffs. ¹³ Yet Pharaoh's heart became hard and he would not listen to them, just as the Lord had said.

The Plague of Blood

¹⁴ Then the Lord said to Moses, "Pharaoh's heart is unyielding; he refuses to let the people go. ¹⁵ Go to Pharaoh in the morning as he goes out to the river. Confront him on the bank of the Nile, and take in your hand the staff that was changed into a snake. ¹⁶ Then say to him, 'The Lord, the God of the Hebrews, has sent me to say to you:

Let my people go, so that they may worship me in the wilderness. But until now you have not listened. ¹⁷ This is what the Lord says: By this you will know that I am the Lord: With the staff that is in my hand I will strike the water of the Nile, and it will be changed into blood. ¹⁸ The fish in the Nile will die, and the river will stink; the Egyptians will not be able to drink its water.'"

¹⁹ The Lord said to Moses, "Tell Aaron, 'Take your staff and stretch out your hand over the waters of Egypt— over the streams and canals, over the ponds and all the reservoirs—and they will turn to blood.' Blood will be everywhere in Egypt, even in vessels^[a] of wood and stone."

²⁰ Moses and Aaron did just as the Lord had commanded. He raised his staff in the presence of Pharaoh and his officials and struck the water of the Nile, and all the water was changed into blood. ²¹ The fish in the Nile died, and the river smelled so bad that the Egyptians could not drink its water. Blood was everywhere in Egypt.

²² But the Egyptian magicians did the same things by their secret arts, and Pharaoh's heart became hard; he would not listen to Moses and Aaron, just as the Lord had said. ²³ Instead, he turned and went into his palace, and did not take even this to his heart. ²⁴ And all the Egyptians dug along the Nile to get drinking water, because they could not drink the water of the river"

My fellow brothers and sisters did we just realized in the above scriptures; that almost all the miracles, signs and wonders the prophecies that God made prophet Moses performed, Pharaoh also made his prophets and magicians performed the same or similar miracles, signs and wonders.

Now precious one, can you bare with me that we shouldn't focus or we should be much careful of what is going on in today's churches about prophets and their prophecies.

Again I am not speaking against prophets and prophecies but am making us to be aware that we have and we must pray to God for him to give us the testing spirits for us to be able to test any prophet or any man who claim to be a man from God.

For we are the ones in danger but not God, i know very well that a false prophet can prophecy to you in the name of God, Jesus, Holy Spirit even go further to say angels brought them the message but they will be lying, may the lord help us.

In addition let's look at another story from the Bible to clarify what I am writing about...

(1KINGS 13:1-13)

AND BEHOLD, there came a man of God out of Judah by the word of the Lord to Bethel. Jeroboam stood by the altar to burn incense. The Man cried against the altar by the word of the Lord, O altar, altar thus says the Lord: Behold, a son shall be born to the house of David, Josiah by name; and on you shall he offer the priests of the high places who burn incense on you, and men's bones shall be burned on you. And he gave a sign the same day, saying, This is the sign which the Lord has spoken: Behold, the altar shall be split and the ashes that are upon it shall be poured out. [Fulfilled in II Kings 23:15,16]. When King Jeroboam heard the words the man of God cried against the altar in Bethel, he thrust out his hand, saying, Lay hold on him! And his hand which he put forth against him dried up, so that he could not draw it to him again. The altar also was split and the ashes poured out from the altar according to the sign which the man of God had given by the word of the Lord. And the kind said to the man of God, Entreat now the favor of the Lord your God and pray for me, that my hand may be restored to me. And the man of God entreated the Lord, and the King's hand was restored and became as it was before. And the king said to the man of God, Come home with me and refresh yourself, and I will give you a reward. And the man of God said to the king, If you give me half your house, I will go in with you, and I will not eat bread or drink water in this place, For I was commanded by the word of the Lord, You shall eat no bread or drink water or return by the way you came, So he went another way and did not return by the way that he came to Bethel. Now there dwelt

*an old prophet in Bethel; and his sons came and told him
all that the man of God had done that day in Bethel; the
words which he had spoken to the king they told also to
their father. Their father asked them, Which way did he
go? For his sons had seen which way the man of God who
came from Judah had gone. He said to his sons, Saddle
the donkey for me. So they saddled the donkey and he rode
on it".*

Oh my gracious God! With the above scriptures can we just testify this revelation ourselves? It speaks of everything and anything I am writing about. How powerful the Holy Spirit is with this awesome revelation. I pray for our merciful lord should have mercy on us for we are ignorant of so many things and now allowing ourselves to be deceived by false prophets.

Children of God, looking at the story from the above scriptures, I believe no one can dispute the fact that the man from Judah from the beginning of the verse wasn't a true man from God, with the miracles and prophecies he declared on the alter and the great signs and wonders that followed and even when the king ordered, that the people should seized him because he was truly sent from God, the hand of the king he stretched towards the man of God became shriveled (leprosy).

Jesus! This is powerful, everything this man of God proclaimed came to pass as the lord made him said to the king and his people but just see how (Satan) the enemy also performed through an Old Prophet right after this man of God (Prophet) have delivered what God has sent him to do.

We noticed from the story that an Older Prophet who heard of what this man of God has done in the Presence of the King and the people of that town, This old prophet whose name wasn't mention in the Bible got jealous when his children brought him the news about the true man of God who was said to come from Judah but his name too wasn't mentioned.

People of God, this Old Prophet saddled his donkey quickly because I believe jealousy over took him and he had been in that same town but had not been able to performed like that in the presence of the king, though He was a prophet of God but maybe

27

God had not use him or sent him like that before. And he had not been given the attention that he needed in that town or no one even remembered nor recognized him, he wasn't fame and don't even get gift from the king or no one even offers him anything not even welcome him to eat in people's houses and homes.

Brothers and Sisters even if it was you, you will get jealous for another prophet from a different town to come into your town to perform or do what you can not do whilst you are all prophets.

Precious one you see, like I said earlier that people go to consult fetish, occultism and smaller Gods to perform prophecies, miracles, signs and wonders which are not from God. Why? Because of jealousy, wealth, greediness, envies, wants to do better than this man of God or that man of God, live luxury lives, buy mansions and expensive cars and even private jets.

Today because of life anxieties, men of God and Prophets are fighting over wealth; they want to gain everything of the world, going through competition upon competitions among themselves.

Because of this, they organize programs upon programs to deceive people with program titles Like; Billionaires Conferences, seven (7) days or twenty one (21) days prophetic impartation, three (3) days or seven (7) days Power Packed miracles, prophecies and sign and wonders.

People of God have you sit down a minute to ponder about this because everything about this program has got to do with money, success, prosperity, riches, wealth and because they want to live good and luxury lives.

This is exactly what prophet Isaiah declared in the book of... (Isaiah 56:11)

> *"They are dogs with mighty appetites they never have enough, they are shepherd who lack understanding; they all turn to their own way and each seeks his own gain".*

Please I am not sayings is not good to be rich or be prosperous but try and understand that this is blinding us from the end times, the coming of Jesus Christ, we too have focus on gaining wealth and what we will eat, drink and wear rather than salvation.

"For *the kingdom of God is not a matter of eating and drinking but of righteousness, peace and joy in the Holy Spirit.*"

(Romans 14:17)

You can even testify that certain program titles are very funny and because we are also not having the spirit of descentment and ascendment to testify or verify from God we packed ourselves with our family to certain programs. You just imagine programs like three (3) days or seven (7) days power packed prophetic declarations. In fact this is lack of knowledge and we are perishing.

Believers try to bear with me that; isn't the power of God that brought creation into existence, isn't the power of God that made the universe and is even the power of God that brought Jesus Christ into the world.

Now brothers and sisters the power of God which is stronger, heavier, higher and greater than ourselves and anything of this world this power can now be packed in three (3) days or seven (7) days prophetic conferences. Please I think we should pray for God himself to help us with his supernatural gifting's for our spirits to be sensitive with such professional lies with these program and conference titles, for the devil is an educated liar, Thank you Holy Spirit for this deeper, higher and greater insight.

Now to continue with the above story about the man of God from Judea and the old prophet, it happened that the old prophet got jealous, saddle his donkey and traced the man of God from Judea.

Because he was told that the king even offered him gift, food and drink in his house but the man of God refused to eat and rejected the gifts.

The old prophet came to meet the man of God sitting down under an oak tree relaxing. And the old prophet asked *"are you the man of God from Judea"*. Precious one if this old prophet claims he is a prophet of God why is he asking of the man's personality or identity, he didn't know or God never told him already. Again he said to the man of God, I want to you to come and eat, drink and rest in my house and after that you can continue your journey the next day or to where you are going.

The man of God rejected his offer by telling him that God have warned him not to eat, drink in that town also shouldn't go on the direction he came from. But the older prophet said to the man of God *"me too am a prophet and an angel from God have come to tell me in my dream that I should bring you to my house and offer you food, drink and rest for you must be very tired"*. -But this old prophet was lying.

People of God you also see that a prophet can use the name of the Lord to lie, that is why the bible said,it isn't every one that uses the name of the lord will be getting into his kingdom or is from God.

> *"Not everyone who says to me lord, lord; will enter the kingdom of heaven but only he who does the will of my father who is in heaven".*

(Matthew 7:21)

We should just imagine what a prophet can do to another prophet how much more to the congregation.

Please be aware of this; that false prophets don't even care about your souls how you are going to perish, all they focus on is to gain fame, wealth, luxury and drive you into destructions with their fake and false prophesies for your souls to perish in hell because they are sent from Satan.

Please if we don't want our souls to perish then I am pleading with you to rather look or listen to the preachers that preach of repentance (revelation), end times to gain the procedure of forgiveness (atonement) which is going to help us confess our sins to be able to receive the Holy Spirit in our lives.

Beloved, listen to another revelation from the same story of the man of God from Judea and the old Prophet.

Did we realized that the man of God from Judea put his blessings out there by telling the Old Prophet that *God say's I shouldn't eat, drink and even I am not to go on the direction I came from.*

In fact if this man of God have not spoken this to the Old Prophet and just refused his offer, trust me there is no way his distraction would have come. But by speaking of the secret and the direction God have told him to follow brought him destruction instead of blessings.

Therefore children of God imagine if the devil should hear or overhears your Blessings in you or on your life Spoken or declared to you by a prophet, what do you think will happen to you or your life? The devil will by all means become conscious of you and your blessings and you are going to be his target until he hunts you down and brings you to eternal destruction. Why will you then be depending on prophets and their prophetic decrees before you survive whilst you don't even know they are from God.

Please let me share with you a very appetizing story for you to tap into your thoughts so you can start thinking of the Lord and his truthfulness...

(Genesis 27:1-35)

When Isaac was old and his eyes were so weak that he could no longer see, he called for Esau his older son and said to him, "My son."

"Here I am," he answered.

² Isaac said, "I am now an old man and don't know the day of my death. ³ Now then, get your equipment—your quiver and bow—and go out to the open country to hunt some wild game for me. ⁴ prepare me the kind of tasty food I like and bring it to me to eat, so that I may give you my blessing before I die."

⁵ Now Rebekah was listening as Isaac spoke to his son Esau. When Esau left for the open country to hunt game and bring it back, ⁶ Rebekah said to her son Jacob, "Look, I overheard your father say to your brother Esau, ⁷ 'Bring me some game and prepare me some tasty food to eat, so that I may give you my blessing in the presence of the Lord before I die.' ⁸ Now, my son, listen carefully and do what I tell you: ⁹ Go out to the flock and bring me two choice young goats, so I can prepare some tasty food for your father, just the way he likes it. ¹⁰ *Then take it to your father to eat, so that he may give you his blessing before he dies."*

¹¹ *Jacob said to Rebekah his mother, "But my brother Esau is a hairy man while I have smooth skin.* ¹² *What if my father touches me? I would appear to be tricking him and would bring down a curse on myself rather than a blessing."*

¹³ *His mother said to him, "My son, let the curse fall on me. Just do what I say; go and get them for me."*

¹⁴ *So he went and got them and brought them to his mother, and she prepared some tasty food, just the way his father liked it.* ¹⁵ *Then Rebekah took the best clothes of Esau her older son, which she had in the house, and put them on her younger son Jacob.* ¹⁶ *She also covered his hands and the smooth part of his neck with the goatskins.* ¹⁷ *Then she handed to her son Jacob the tasty food and the bread she had made.*

¹⁸ *He went to his father and said, "My father."*

"Yes, my son," he answered. "Who is it?"

19 Jacob said to his father, "I am Esau your firstborn. I have done as you told me. Please sit up and eat some of my game, so that you may give me your blessing."

20 Isaac asked his son, "How did you find it so quickly, my son?"

"The Lord your God gave me success," he replied.

21 Then Isaac said to Jacob, "Come near so I can touch you, my son, to know whether you really are my son Esau or not."

22 Jacob went close to his father Isaac, who touched him and said, "The voice is the voice of Jacob, but the hands are the hands of Esau." 23 He did not recognize him, for his hands were hairy like those of his brother Esau; so he proceeded to bless him. 24 "Are you really my son Esau?" he asked "I am," he replied.

25 Then he said, "My son, bring me some of your game to eat, so that I may give you my blessing."

Jacob brought it to him and he ate; and he brought some wine and he drank. 26 Then his father Isaac said to him, "Come here, my son, and kiss me."

27 So he went to him and kissed him. When Isaac caught the smell of his clothes, he blessed him and said,
"Ah, the smell of my son
is like the smell of a field
that the Lord has blessed.

28 May God give you heaven's dew
and earth's richness—
an abundance of grain and new wine.

29 May nations serve you
and peoples bow down to you.

Be lord over your brothers,
and may the sons of your mother bow down to you.

May those who curse you be cursed
and those who bless you be blessed."

30 After Isaac finished blessing him, and Jacob had scarcely left his father's presence, his brother Esau came in from hunting. 31 He too prepared some tasty food and brought it to his father. Then he said to him, "My father, please sit up and eat some of my game, so that you may give me your blessing."

32 His father Isaac asked him, "Who are you?"

"I am your son," he answered, "your firstborn, Esau."

33 Isaac trembled violently and said, "Who was it, then, that hunted game and brought it to me? I ate it just before you came and I blessed him—and indeed he will be blessed!"

34 When Esau heard his father's words, he burst out with a loud and bitter cry and said to his father, "Bless me— me too, my father!"

35 But he said, "Your brother came deceitfully and took your blessing."

People of God, we should just understand that this revelation is truly from the Holy Spirit, can we imagine deliberately what took place when Rebekah over heard that Isaac wants to Bless Esau.

We should just imagine that Isaac was a prophet and was speaking to Esau, yes! In deed Isaac was also a prophet of God.

Believers the Bible declares that Rebekah gradually and bitterly turned the blessings around by switching Jacob to be Essau and at the end of it all the blessings was stolen from Essau.

People of God I know biblically this was how it was supposed to be but imagine if the devil overhears your blessings – what God wants to do for you in the future. The devil will by all means fight your blessings and destruct you, for you to go through struggle and what you must use only one day to receive it will take you one year or more to receive it.

> *"Jacob lived in the land where his father had stayed, the land of Canaan.*
>
> *² This is the account of Jacob's family line.*
>
> *Joseph, a young man of seventeen, was tending the flocks with his brothers, the sons of Bilhah and the sons of Zilpah, his father's wives, and he brought their father a bad report about them.*
>
> *³ Now Israel loved Joseph more than any of his other sons, because he had been born to him in his old age; and he made an ornate[a] robe for him. ⁴ When his brothers saw that their father loved him more than any of them, they hated him and could not speak a kind word to him.*
>
> *⁵ Joseph had a dream, and when he told it to his brothers, they hated him all the more. ⁶ He said to them, "Listen to this dream I had: ⁷ We were binding sheaves of grain out in the field when suddenly my sheaf rose and stood upright, while your sheaves gathered around mine and bowed down to it."*

⁸ His brothers said to him, "Do you intend to reign over us? Will you actually rule us?" And they hated him all the more because of his dream and what he had said.

⁹ Then he had another dream, and he told it to his brothers. "Listen," he said, "I had another dream, and this time the sun and moon and eleven stars were bowing down to me."

¹⁰ When he told his father as well as his brothers, his father rebuked him and said, "What is this dream you had? Will your mother and I and your brothers actually come and bow down to the ground before you?"

(Genesis 37:1-10)

Another story about Joseph from the bible gives us a clear revelation of Joseph speaking his blessings out to his family through his vision (Dreams) about what God is planning to do for him in the future.

Beloved, from that day Joseph made a mistake to speak out his blessings for the Devil to overhear him; Joseph went through a time of bitterness, struggle and agony before he achieved his goals in life, I pray that may the Lord continue to help us.

May the Lord frustrate the plans of our enemies and what ever they are planning against us if the devil or his demons have overheard our blessings of what God is planning to do for his children in the future?

Or else the blessings we need only one day for it to be fulfilled can take or is going to take several days' even years.

Please let me elaborate on this with the story of Jacob after he run away from home with the blessings of his blood brother Esau.

"Now Laban had two daughters; the name of the older was Leah, and the name of the younger was Rachel. ¹⁷ Leah had weak[a] eyes, but Rachel had a lovely figure and was beautiful. ¹⁸ Jacob was in love with Rachel and said, "I'll work for you seven years in return for your younger daughter Rachel."

¹⁹ Laban said, "It's better that I give her to you than to some other man. Stay here with me." ²⁰ So Jacob served seven years to get Rachel, but they seemed like only a few days to him because of his love for her.

²¹ Then Jacob said to Laban, "Give me my wife. My time is completed, and I want to make love to her."

²² So Laban brought together all the people of the place and gave a feast. ²³ But when evening came, he took his daughter Leah and brought her to Jacob, and Jacob made love to her. ²⁴ And Laban gave his servant Zilpah to his daughter as her attendant.

²⁵ When morning came, there was Leah! So Jacob said to Laban, "What is this you have done to me? I served you for Rachel, didn't I? Why have you deceived me?"

²⁶ Laban replied, "It is not our custom here to give the younger daughter in marriage before the older one. ²⁷ Finish this daughter's bridal week; then we will give you the younger one also, in return for another seven years of work."

²⁸ And Jacob did so. He finished the week with Leah, and then Laban gave him his daughter Rachel to be his wife. ²⁹ Laban gave his servant Bilhah to his daughter Rachel as her attendant. ³⁰ Jacob made love to Rachel also, and his love for Rachel was greater than his love for Leah. And he worked for Laban another seven years.

(Genesis 29:16-30)

The bible declares that Jacob ran to stayed with his Uncle Laban, Rebekah's brother. Then it got to a time that Jacob wants to marry Rachel the second daughter of his Uncle Laban but he has to serve for seven years before Jacob can marry Rachel, the bible declares that, Jacob was able to serve for that seven (7) years and they performed the marriage rights as if it was between Jacob and Rachel but during the evening Rachel was switch to Leah Laban's first daughter.

And the next morning when Jacob realized it wasn't Rachel but Leah, he approached Laban but Laban said to him "*in our family the oldest must marry first before the youngest*".

So Jacob agreed to serve for another seven (7) years to have Rachel.

What a pity! People of God and the bible also declare that Laban was an Idol worshiper (wizard).

This is dangerous in our world and this tells you that when the devil knows your story or your blessings he will consciously and strategically put you through all sought of struggle to bring your destruction and what you will use only one day to achieve it will take you several years to achieve them.

Brother and Sisters, in fact this book is very awesome and the revelation the Holy Spirit is releasing to us is very powerful. What I can say is that Prophecy is good and it's very encouraging in the body of Jesus Christ but at the same time God is telling us to be vigilant of false prophets in this Endtimes.

And this is totally true from the Spirit of God, because imagine a prophet is prophesying unto your life and he begin by telling you your bank accounts numbers; don't you think he is trying to help the devil over hears your finances. When he prophecy by telling you your names and home addresses including your telephone numbers, beloved trust me if the devil should over hears your details like this he will and can trace you, locate you without a miss.

People of God to be precise, what has bank account numbers, names, telephone numbers and address of your various homes and houses got to do with repentance, confession of your sins and experiencing the Holy Spirit baptism to be able to walk in holiness? Because the heartbeat of God is to preach, repentance, end times, confession and Holy Spirit baptism.

We must know and understand that God had great and greater prophets from the beginning of the bible and to be honest it wasn't in this form, kind and manner of performing. They were prophets that spoke of the revelation of the endtimes, the coming of Jesus Christ the son of man.

They were delivering exactly what God had told them to deliver, beloved God is a secret God and he doesn't tell people secretes like that until is needed and is going to benefit him and his kingdom.

We should remember the story of Jesus Christ when he asked a Samaritan woman to give him water to drink.

"Now Jesus learned that the Pharisees had heard that he was gaining and baptizing more disciples than John—
² although it was not Jesus who baptized, but his disciples.
³ So he left Judea and went back once more to Galilee.

⁴ Now he had to go through Samaria. ⁵ So he came to a town in Samaria called Sychar, near the plot of ground Jacob had given to his son Joseph. ⁶ Jacob's well was there, and Jesus, tired as he was from the journey, sat down by the well. It was about noon.

⁷ When a Samaritan woman came to draw water, Jesus said to her, "Will you give me a drink?" ⁸ (His disciples had gone into the town to buy food.)

⁹ The Samaritan woman said to him, "You are a Jew and I am a Samaritan woman. How can you ask me for a drink?" (For Jews do not associate with Samaritans.[a])

¹⁰ Jesus answered her, "If you knew the gift of God and who it is that asks you for a drink, you would have asked him and he would have given you living water."

¹¹ "Sir," the woman said, "you have nothing to draw with and the well is deep. Where can you get this living water? ¹² Are you greater than our father Jacob, who gave us the well and drank from it himself, as did also his sons and his livestock?"

¹³ Jesus answered, "Everyone who drinks this water will be thirsty again, ¹⁴ but whoever drinks the water I give them will never thirst. Indeed, the water I give them will become in them a spring of water welling up to eternal life."

¹⁵ The woman said to him, "Sir, give me this water so that I won't get thirsty and have to keep coming here to draw water."

16 He told her, "Go, call your husband and come back."

17 "I have no husband," she replied. Jesus said to her, "You are right when you say you have no husband. 18 The fact is, you have had five husbands, and the man you now have is not your husband. What you have just said is quite true."

19 "Sir," the woman said, "I can see that you are a prophet. 20 Our ancestors worshiped on this mountain, but you Jews claim that the place where we must worship is in Jerusalem."

21 "Woman," Jesus replied, "believe me, a time is coming when you will worship the Father neither on this mountain nor in Jerusalem. 22 You Samaritans worship what you do not know; we worship what we do know, for salvation is from the Jews. 23 Yet a time is coming and has now come when the true worshipers will worship the Father in the Spirit and in truth, for they are the kind of worshipers the Father seeks. 24 God is spirit, and his worshipers must worship in the Spirit and in truth."

25 The woman said, "I know that Messiah" (called Christ) "is coming. When he comes, he will explain everything to us."

26 Then Jesus declared, "I, the one speaking to you—I am he."

(John 4:1-26)

Precious one, look how fascinating this story of Jesus Christ is; Jesus was claimed to be of prophet by the Samaritan woman when Jesus said to her that she have had five (5) husbands, and the man she is even having now is not her husband.

In fact Jesus was indeed a prophet. And I want you to for a second analyzed something; Jesus Christ said to the women you have had five (5) husbands, and would you believe me that Jesus at that time will by all means know their names, and he can even tell the woman of her house location and everything but that was none of his business, all He cared about was for this woman to know what is repentance, salvation and eternal life.

Isn't this great, simple and powerful than to put fear in the people to bring out their details out there for the enemy to be aware of it and begin to chase after peoples destiny.

Beloved, one thing we must know and understand is, God is omnipotent, omnipresent and omniscient. Which means God is everywhere and he knows everything in our life's both past, present and future.

But the devil doesn't know anything and he is not everywhere also, the bible declarer's that the devil roars like a lion, looking for someone to devour.

"Be alert and of sober mind. Your enemy the devil prowls around like a roaring lion looking for someone to devour."

(1 peter 5:8)

This verse means that the devil searches for stuff, products and peoples details to base on and used it to hunt for souls. Therefore precious one, why this too much prophecies of unnecessary information about people and putting poor souls into trouble in most churches and many prophetic conferences being held in the world today.

You know, God is the owner of the universe and everything in it therefore he doesn't need to give you too much evidence and prove before you realized He is God. Everything in us, on us, with us and around us speaks of how great and powerful our almighty God is.

Besides Jesus Christ tells us that, the Spirit that brings prophecies to us for prophets to speak them is going to function. The Spirit will tells us the things of the future, the Spirit is the Spirit of truth and He is going to only tells us exactly what he hears from God.

Beloved I believed you have marveled and you are very happy of knowing this today.

In fact this is a deep revelation for us to know what is needed from God's messengers; When Jesus Christ was being taken to heaven, the massage he wanted us to go out to the world to *preach* is about the good news.

He said we should all preach, but didn't say some should prophecy and some should baptize people.

And he really needed us to preach what is going to help his kingdom benefit, he needed us to win souls and help them in the Baptizm of the Holy Spirit which is the only way for one to walk in holiness and have eternal salvation.

But we should look at what our preachers have turned into in the world today everything is prophecy, prophetic and prophetic directions. Yes, I agree that prophecy and it directions are good but of what good will it be when at the end you will be blessed but will go to hell.

Please many prophets don't care about your soul because they are not from God, all they want is your money to live a life of luxury, become famous and gain wealth by making you sowing prophetic seed and consecrated seeds to them. Please we should be very careful of today's prophets for the bible speaks of false prophets getting to the endtimes. And it is easy for people and everyone to prophecy because is all about phone numbers, bank account numbers, names and home addresses.

Beloved, before telephone numbers and bank account numbers were not available in the universe weren't there prophets and prophecies but because it has become fun and entertaining, every one wants to prophecy telephone numbers, names, date of births, home addressed to surprise the congregation for the church to know how powerful they are.

Please we should rather be sad but not surprise because when they mention your private details like that they put fear in you and plant corruption in your mind so when they tells you to bring anything in the form of money or luxury they already know you have them so they will by all means snatch what you have from you. And because they have put fear in you, you will be more afraid not to do what they will instruct or direct you to do.

But I declare to you that mentioning or giving some one phone numbers and bank account numbers doesn't make you more powerful than telling someone to go into the sea, catch a fish and bring out money out of that fish to settle your taxes and debts.

Precious one, prophecy's and the gift of prophecy is good because I am much aware that getting to the endtimes God is going to release gifts upon spiritual gifts to people some are visions, dreams, prophecies and others.

"in the last days God says I will pour out my spirit on all people, your sons and daughters will prophesy, your young men will see visions, your old men will dream dreams, even on my servants both men and women I will pour out my spirit in those days and they will prophesy".

(Acts 2:17-18)

but at the same time God is also telling us that we should be aware of it that the devil will realize this and try to be smart, he will try to use this same gift as an advantage over God's children to pull souls to him self.

And he is going to do this through false prophecy he will make it look fun and entertaining for even souls of Jesus Christ to enjoy and be enticed by it. Thus why the bible declares that; if those days had not been shortened, there will be no one to be saved because of what is happening today. Even the elect souls of God will be deceived.

Prophecy is good but it gives birth to two things is either by direction or destruction which by explaining earlier, how people and men of God got directed and at the same time destructed by prophecies.

For me I keep on asking myself the same question again and again that why is Jesus Christ so particular about false prophets that will appear to deceive many, even his chosen ones will be deceived through false prophecies with their false miracles, signs and wonders.

"For false Christ and false prophets will appear and perform great signs and miracles to deceive even the elect – if that were possible".

(Matthew 24:24)

I believe that in the world today if you are not a prophet or cannot prophecy you are not received or accepted or welcome in other minister's church to preach. Because everyone is enticed by prophecies, prophets and their prophetic words but you know God didn't use prophets like that in the olden days. It wasn't every day that God speaks through them to people and they were not even sure of God speaking to them at particular times.

But with prophets of today, they can and will assure you prophetic word from the Lord. How are they sure whether God is going to speak about something or someone through them when they go about organizing programs and promising people to come to their conferences for a prophetic word or various types of prophecies?

In fact this is dangerous, ridiculous and are insult to God and his Kingdom for people to allow themselves to be deceived about false prophecies because if we should be careful and watchful to this prophets we will know that all what is of them is false. Because you can't assure or promise God's Prophetic word to people, but why are they doing this? Is because they want to be received, accepted, gain fame, wealth and live luxury lives.

I remember that a man of God one's told me that before he could go and preach in a church, the church that invited him have to put half of the amount he will charge into his accounts and after he has finish preaching or after the program they will give him the balance. And this is not just done by only him but this is a principle between men and women of God in the world today.

So if you are a man or a woman of God and you don't enjoy what this other men and women of God are enjoying then why won't you also do what you have to do to be counted among this men and women of God by following their lead so you can be invited to churches and be able to travel around the Globe to globalized the prophecies you have installed by your own means.

But my question is, are you doing or are they doing this by the authority of Jesus Christ or through the Holy Spirit. That is all we should also ask ourselves for the devil came to steal, kill and destroy our souls, and if you are a man or a woman of God and because of prophecies or prophetic word and you are inviting prophets and prophetess into your church to come and prophecy then I guess you have to be careful and test their spirit to see whether they are from God.

Because the bible declares that they are wolves in sheep clothing (skin) this makes it very difficult to see them through nature until the Holy Spirit reveals their true nature to you.

> *"Watch out for false prophets they come to you in sheep's clothing, but inwardly they are ferocious wolves, by their fruit you will recognize them".*

(Matthew 7:15-16.)

This means definitely they will deceive true and genuine men and women of God, which is even happening in the world today, so I urge you to be more prayerful and seek the guidance and the direction of the Holy Spirit. We should watch out and pray without season.

> *"Watch and pray so that you will not fall into temptation; the spirit is willing but the body is weak."*

(Matthew 26:41)

So we cannot be tempted and deceived for this false prophets and what the Anti-Christ will be doing in the world will be very enticing, entertaining and very attractive to deceive strong souls of God.

This is what the bible is alerting us so we take note of it, because a thief cannot go into a strong man's house to steal until the thief ties the strong man before he or she can steal the possessions of the strong man.

> *"But no one can enter a strong man's house and plunder his goods, unless he first binds the strong man. Then indeed he may plunder his house".*

(Mark 3:27)

Therefore this is what the false prophets are doing, they will entice you with entertaining prophecies, names telephone numbers, and surprise you with your bank accounts numbers to attract your attention and get to your Soul by beginning to prophecy God's blessings on your soul and because they were right and correct when they mentioned your names, telephone numbers and surprised you with your bank details and your house information's you might surly believe that the blessing of God which they are prophesying on your life is perfectly true and convincingly it comes from God but little would you know that your soul has been stolen to eternal destruction.

Now let me give you a clue of what you need to understand because it makes sense – now why should a prophet or someone tell you bank details, telephone numbers and personal information of you; and you are surprise and believe that he is genuine, this is our lack of knowledge and wisdom because it is possible for them to tell you what you already have but what about what you don't have.

Why is it that before you never had a car number or a phone number they never came in to tell you that tomorrow by this time or a year by this time you will have a phone number, a car number or a bank accounts number like this or that but now that you already have it they are telling you what you already have and done by the lords power and blessings he has given to you.

Please this sounds good and I want you to meditate on it, this should tell us that the devil knows only what has already been done but doesn't know what is of you in the future.

Have you thought of it this way, supposing you have no bank accounts, telephone numbers and personal details what are they going to tell you. These prophets are telling you what is possible but what about the impossible, let them tell you what you don't already have and the things that seems impossible to you. Because that is what Jesus Christ will do he will rather surprise you with the impossible ones.

Most of the blame will be giving to the true and genuine prophets from God because they might be real prophets of God but the devil have offered them the pleasure, wealth, luxury and riches of the world which they couldn't resist it and now they are dancing to the music of the devil (Satan).

The devil is very intelligent because as he hide behind the biblical words to try to deceive Jesus Christ the son of God, so as he is hiding behind all the prosperity, blessing and wealth messages from God and Jesus Christ in the Bible to deceive true prophets, men and women of God today for too much of everything is bad and we should realized that the Bible speaks to us that on that day many men and woman of God will ask God *"we preached prophecy, perform miracle, signs and wonders in your name"* But. God will reply them that *"he never knew them"*.

> *"Many will say to me on that day lord, lord did we not prophesy in your name drive out demons and perform many miracles? Then I will tell them plainly, I never knew you, away from, you evildoers".*

(Matthew 7:22-23)

People of God, could you believe that based on this facts; many Prophets are setting up and have set up prophetic schools where people purposely go there to learn prophecy.

Prophecies are now being thought in schools and People are being thought how to prophecy, the strategies and the systematic way to prophecy to people to know what they are revealing about your details is true.

But I want you to ask yourself that after your information or details have been mentioned by a prophet what is the real message God have told him to tell you.

I pray that may the lord bless us with wisdom and knowledge to be vigilant and careful about true men of God and false prophets.

This also draws my mind back to a story in the bible from the Old Testament in the book of...

(2 CHRONICLES 18:17-27)

> *And King [Ahab] of Israel said to Jehoshaphat, Did I not tell you that he would not prophesy good to me, but evil? [Micaiah] said, Therefore hear the word of the Lord: I saw the Lord sitting on His throne, and all the host of*

heaven standing at His right hand and His left. And the Lord said, Who Shall entice Ahab king of Isreal, that he may go up and fall at Ramoth – gilead? And one said this thing, and another that, Then there came a spirit and stood before the Lord and said, I will entice him. The Lord said to him. By what means? And he said, I will go out and be a lying spirit in the mouths of all his prophets. And the Lord said, You shall entice him and also succeed. Go forth and do so. Now, you see, the Lord put a lying spirit in the mouths of your prophets; and the Lord has spoken evil concerning you. The Zedekiah the son of Chenaanah came hear and smote Micaiah upon the cheek and said, Which way went the Spirit of the Lord from me to speak to you? And Micaiah said, Behold, you shall see on that day when you shall go into an inner chamber to hide yourself. That King [Ahab] of Israel said, take Micaiah back to Amon the governor of the city and to Joash the king's son. And say, thus says the king: Put this fellow in prison and feed him with bread and water of affliction until I return in peace. Micaiah said, If you return at all in peace, the Lord has not spoken by me. And he added; hear it, you people, all of you!

In fact people of God, the above scripture is a very powerful message, I believe it speaks to you directly.

Could you believe that a king is going to war and he decided to inquire of the Lord, so quickly they gathered for him four hundred (400) prophets and the bible declares that they all prophecy to the same thing but the king wasn't sure and satisfied with their prophecies so he again asked, *"is there any prophet of the Lord around"*.

Precious one this is very unbelievable, now the king requested for a prophet from the Lord therefore where are the four hundred (400) prophets from? Are they not from the Lord? This means there are some Prophets from the Lord that are truly genuine and others are not, with my understanding of this story; I believe that some prophets prophecy to please people, the church and to be accepted and gain fame and wealth.

But the prophets from the Lord speak the truth not to please mankind but to please God. They only speak of what they hear from God through the Holy Spirit.

Believers please this is a very strong revelation I want you to meditate on it, ask your self-question; why everybody in the church or every leader in the church wants to prophecy and trust me many of them are prophesying the same thing repeatedly.

Everyone is prophesying names, telephone numbers, and bank account numbers and giving personal and private details of the people in the church to be overhead either by the people or the devil (Satan).

Friends do you believe that when a prophet prophecy to you the devil overhears it too? And what do you think will happen; he becomes conscious of you and begins to torment your life and the blessings upon your destiny.

Believe me; many people are learning how to prophecy in the church today so the devil has realized the weak points of the church. So why won't he also present and preserve himself to the church or in the church as a prophet because the churches don't focus on the power to distinguish between prophets who are from the Lord and prophet who are not.

Men and women of God reading this book, i want you to be enticed by the revelation, insight and foresight in this book to be cautious of what is happening in the church or in the world today and begin to preach the good news to the church, preach repentance, end times and let the them be convicted of their sins, they should regret and seek repentance so you can teach them the process or the procedure of how they can be forgiven by God almighty which is done by one's confessing of his or her sins.

Precious one, just only confess, speak, say your sins to God and let him know how ignorant you are but now you have regret and you are turning to him.

Then, after that you will and can begin to understand the Holy Spirit to receive his baptism through faith by believing that Jesus Christ is the son of God. Because people of God the devil is winning, drawing and attracting souls through the fancy and entertaining Prophets and their prophecies in the world today.

And even if there are true prophets of the Lord, how can we or how are we going to distinguish between this prophets. Because they are all prophesying the same thing in the church today, but the true word of God which is the good news is missing in the church. Repentance, salvation and Holy Spirit Baptism, revelation of the end time's messages are all missing today people of God.

Many are the ones who are writing books of how to prophecy, how to protect prophecy, how to make prophetic decrees and declarations through prayer, how to gain prophetic keys and so-on.

People of God I am not saying this or some of this things are not good and true but please we should read the Bible and analyzed things, pray for the **Holy Spirit** to reveal the truth to us. We should rather depend on preaching's and prophecies which its foundation is of the truth from the bible.

You know the word of the lord is like a hammer that breaks a mighty rock into pieces.

Therefore if God speaks, believe me it breaks Boundaries and limitations and nothing, absolutely nothing can hinder it and you shall be blessed no matter who you are where you are and it doesn't matter how long it delays or waits you shall be blessed and accomplish what God wants you to accomplish.

But here in this case in to today's world before you receive a prophecy from a prophet you have to sow a prophetic seed to make it come to pass. Yes, I believe these are prophetic directions and some are biblical but how would you know or testify that the prophet standing in front of you is a true prophet from the Lord.

Precious one at this point I urge you to be fervent in your prayers and be strengthened by the Holy Spirit to read the bible and understand what I am trying to share with you.

You know, when I was a child growing up during my time in school and mostly when is time for school break to us to go on vacation. We normally hear speeches' that goes like "*last days are always dangerous*" so we should behave well or else someone might be used as an escape goat.

In fact this is very true and I hope you might or have heard the same thing which is perfectly true and powerful because when Jesus Christ was being taking up to heaven in to mist of his disciples he urged them with this last words

He said we should *go into all ever the world and preach the good news.* I am saying this because we are also his disciples and victims of preaching his good news. Now he furthered by saying we should baptized them when they believe and repent and after that great signs and wonders will follow.

But brothers and Sisters in our world today, People who don't believe in **JESUS CHRIST** and everything about him, are receiving prophecies from various prophets and being touched to receive miracles from God.

> But the bible even declares in the book of Jeremiah the prophet: *"they keep saying to those who despise me, the lord says: you will have peace. And to all who follow the stubbornness of their hearts they say. No harm will come to you. But which of them has stood in council of the Lord to see or to hear his word? Who has listened or heard his word?"*

(Jeremiah 23:17-18)

But believes we should be wise about this if our prophets are not hungry and selfish of being rich, wealthy, successful and wanting to live in luxury.

Why would they prophecy to someone who doesn't believe in God and touched him or her to receive miracles whilst the person doesn't respect and fear God. This is totally false my fellow brothers and sisters, If is not greediness, jealousy and eager to be famous and gain wealth, why on earth won't you preach the good news to the person or the church before miracles, sign, wonders and the blessings of God could follow.

This reminds me of a story a friend of mine shared with me, He said "*he visited a certain church and there were a lot of people, old member, new members and first comers this was a very great church and there was going to be a prophetic service that day with a prophet. So the place was full of members, and during the service the prophet called an elderly woman to come forward and the woman came to stand in front of the congregation then the prophet began to prophecy by speaking the private and personal details of this woman even to the level of telling the woman the conversation she had with the husband before coming to church. But little did the prophet know that this woman is a new member and that day was her first time in a prophetic service besides she was not a repented Christian and doesn't believe and she was very ignorant about Jesus Christ and the gift of prophecy.*

People of God, this woman is not a believer so what and how do you expect her to react. Suddenly, she screamed and got very angry with the prophets that - why is he telling her private and personal details to the congregation and what is the meaning of all this, therefore she is going to call the police to arrest the prophet. And there was destructing spirit in the church every one was destructed, this woman was then calmed down by the congregation and trust me some way somehow this was very embarrassing.

In fact this is exactly what I am saying that Jesus **Christ** wants us to preach the good news and baptized those who believe because many people in the church today are very ignorant of Jesus Christ and how can you prophecy to people who are ignorant about the maker of prophecy.

People of God prophecy are good but the bible declares that to obey is better than sacrifice and the spirit of disobedience is a spirit of divination.

> *"But Samuel replied: does the lord delight in burnt offerings and sacrifices as much as in obeying the voice of the lord? To obey is better than sacrifice, and to heed is better than the fat of rams. For rebellion is like the sin of divination, and arrogance like the evil of idolatry. Because you have rejected the word of the lord he has rejected you as king".*

(1 Samuel 15:22-23).

I know strongly that God would love and like His Children to prophecy but of what benefit will it be to God and His kingdom if we should prophecy to people but their souls are still not won to inherit eternal salvation.

Beloved I keep on saying that prophecy is good and prophets and prophecies are from God and according to the Bible any one whom God speaks through him or her to give messages or deliver messages to his children is a prophet or prophetess. Besides God love prophets and he has made them powerful, Jesus Christ the son of God was a prophet. Therefore I can't by any chance or form or means speak or talk against prophets and the prophecies that God speaks or send through them to give to us his children. Far been from me to speak or write against prophetic because am also a prophet but what I want us to be aware is that Jesus Christ have already warn us his children that getting to the end times the devil will raise through prophets to deceive God's children.

They are going to prophecy as if is from God, they are going to perform great miracles, signs and wonders as if all is from God but it will be a deceiving spirits at the end. The devil will be using these prophets and their false prophecies to deceive people even Christians and draw more souls to his kingdom and send them to eternal destruction.

This is the reason why I am trying to make us understand and be cautious about the word of Jesus Christ the son of God.

Now let me ask this question, why is Jesus Christ warning his children about this particular gift from God, also why is the devil not going to operate and perform in any other gift apart from the *gift of prophecy.*

People of God the greatest answer are because of what is happening in our churches and in the world today. The attractiveness, the fancy and the entertaining part of prophecy is what is stealing, killing and destroying us.

The world love entertainment that is why there are many entertainers in the world today through celebrities, sports, comedy, music, movies and others. In fact the world wants entertainment and needs to be entertained that's why fake prophets and false prophecies are having effects and generating in the church today by chorography, drama, dance and others to the level of even lies prophecies in the church.

I am saying prophecy because our true prophets of today are prophesying names, phone numbers and bank accounts numbers and houses or home addresses. Isn't this entertaining, If a prophet should tell me my date of birth, telephone number, name and some personal details of me for the first time he or she met me in the church or the street isn't this fancy, why won't I take this opportunity to go to more of his programs when he or she invites me.

Children of God, real men and prophets of God today are making entertainment of God's prophecies so the devil find it so easy, very easy to come into the church as a prophet to prophecy and deceive God's children. Because telling people their names, date of birth, phone numbers and bank account numbers are not prophecies.

This thing can be done by fortune tellers; you know there are some people in the world that can just look in your palms and begins to tell you every detail about you. Yes! Fortune tellers they can give you your personal details and this stated from the Old Testament but in the bible they are called *mediums*.

(1 Kings 28:3-11)

People of God the bible even give us a perfect illustration that this kind of performance is sorcery (witchcraft). And this *mediums* what they do is to communicate in the spirit world at times people who are dead. So you see the devil can also win the Christian market by using this type of spirit and disguise himself as a prophet and tell you or your private information and win you to his kingdom. This is no news to the devil, but I ask again what chance or the opportunity has the devil gain to come and operate in the church?

I believe this is because there is no difference of what the prophets are doing in the church and what Satan can do or has done before. People of God we need to be very sensitive to the Holy Spirit and may the lord help us, forgive us and bless our soul and spirit to be spotless and blameless from the second coming of Jesus Christ.

The things we do and think it doesn't mean anything, it means a lot of things in the spiritual world.

Brothers and Sisters if we are truly involve in or with this end times prophets and their prophecies Then I will urge you to read the Bible and learn, sturdy and know more about Gods true prophets how they behaved, their characters and what God wanted and needed his prophets to do.

The Bible truly talks about true prophets and false prophets because God had many prophets and it got to a time the devil involved himself and disguise himself as a false prophet to destruct the instructions God has given to his children and this is the same thing which is happening today in the world.

Many false prophets have merged themselves with true prophets in the church or in the world to destruct the church and draw souls for the devil.

People of God I would love us to go into the Bible and depend on some scriptures and have knowledge about Gods true prophets. God have so many prophets by reading the bible from Abraham to John the baptized and one thing I have really noticed about Gods true prophets from the Bible is; they don't like to take or accept many gifts because some accepted gifts and some rejected gifts from people of high status and even kings.

Reading the bible you will found out that Gods prophets were not leaving in big mansions, houses and owning too much wealth. They were most at time living in the forest, deserts and in caves. They never took to themselves too much and many camels, donkeys and other wealth's. I know some prophets God intentionally blessed them with too much wealth but majority of Gods prophets were living like that of a mad man or like mad men. They were wearing rags, eating unhealthy foods, chewing grass hoppers and being feed by the Ravens.

I believe someone will say that; that was then, which means they were prophets from the old testaments, if so then what about John the Baptist who was a prophet from the New testament and reading about how he portrayed himself and the life he was living was like that of a mad man.

> *"In those days John the Baptist came, preaching in the*
> *wilderness of Judea ² and saying, "Repent, for the kingdom*

of heaven has come near." [3] *This is he who was spoken of through the prophet Isaiah: A voice of one calling in the wilderness, 'Prepare the way for the Lord, make straight paths for him.'"*

[4] *John's clothes were made of camel's hair, and he had a leather belt around his waist. His food was locusts and wild honey.* [5] *People went out to him from Jerusalem and all Judea and the whole region of the Jordan.* [6] *Confessing their sins, they were baptized by him in the Jordan River.*

[7] *But when he saw many of the Pharisees and Sadducees coming to where he was baptizing, he said to them: "You brood of vipers! Who warned you to flee from the coming wrath?* [8] *Produce fruit in keeping with repentance.* [9] *And do not think you can say to yourselves, 'We have Abraham as our father.' I tell you that out of these stones God can raise up children for Abraham.* [10] *The ax is already at the root of the trees, and every tree that does not produce good fruit will be cut down and thrown into the fire.*

[11] *"I baptize you with[b] water for repentance. But after me comes one who is more powerful than I, whose sandals I am not worthy to carry. He will baptize you with[c] the Holy Spirit and fire.* [12] *His winnowing fork is in his hand, and he will clear his threshing floor, gathering his wheat into the barn and burning up the chaff with unquenchable fire."*

(Matthew 3:1-12)

Precious one reading this book I am not saying that richness, wealth and the blessings of God is not true or good and prophets of today should live in poverty; no!, but the prophets of today are falling for too much wealth, too much luxury lives, competition of gaining more than the other. This is what is happening in the world and in the church of today. And the devil has use wealth to blind so many prophets from preaching the good news to the church but rather prophecy to the people to be famous and gain money.

And I want us to understand that is not only prophets specifically that are doing these things many men and women of

God are doing similar thing in the sense that anyone who has been called by God is a prophet or a prophetess.

I want us to understand that anyone whom God uses to preach, prophecy, perform miracles, signs and wonders is a prophet. It shouldn't necessarily means to have the title of a prophet that specifically means you a prophet but any one that God uses as a vessel to send his message to his people is a prophet.

People of God if you could see what am seeing and hear what am hearing in the world and in the church today you will realized that the devil is using and hiding behind riches and wealth to blind many prophets, men and woman of God.

Believers I understand perfectly that is only the blessings of the lord that makes a person rich.

> And also *"the blessing of the lord brings wealth and he adds no trouble to it"*. (Proverbs 10:22).

But can you believe that even Jesus Christ rejected the blessings and the wealth of the devil (Satan). This is when the devil offered Jesus Christ the world if only he can bow to worship him.

> *Again, the devil took him to a very high mountain and showed him all the kingdoms of the world and their splendour.* ⁹ *"All this I will give you," he said, "if you will bow down and worship me."*
>
> ¹⁰ *Jesus said to him, "Away from me, Satan! For it is written: 'Worship the Lord your God, and serve him only.'* ⁱ *Then the devil left him, and angels came and attended him".*
>
> (Matthew 4:8-11).

Precious one can we now understand that the devil also give some people or some men and women of God wealth when they are enticed with the pleasures of the world and gives up to the luxury life of the world. They become corrupted and submissive to the devil yet still will be preaching and acting like their blessing is from God but I declare to you that they are not but why am I saying this.

Is because Jesus Christ was a prophet and even the son of God, but the devil tried to offer him riches and wealth by saying to him "*if only he can worship him, serves him and become his false prophet he will give him the world.* But **Jesus Christ** the true man of God and a true prophet rejected and refused to accept the offer from the devil (Satan).

My Brothers and Sister look at this powerful revelation and try to understand that as a man of God or prophet of God is a must that the devil will come to you to offer you riches, wealth and luxury life in your ministry.

And what I have realized about the men and women of God of today even prophets have fallen for the devil and has been blind by his wealth and riches he has promised and giving them. After this they will pretend that their blessings and wealth is from God but they are lying, that is why the bible is warning us to be careful and vigilant about these prophets because they are false.

And what they will preach about their gains and wealth, they will hide behind the chapter and verses from the bible that proclaims and declares the riches, wealth and the blessings of God to make the church believe that their blessings are from the lord which is a deceiving spirit.

Precious one if the devil (Satan) can offer Jesus Christ who owns the world (Universe) the pleasures in it then why can't he offers it to the followers of Jesus Christ to believe and later be deceived. This is only to use them for his benefit and to draw more souls to himself (Satan) for them to perish in hell.

Based on this revelations I would love us to be careful be more vigilant and analyze what is going on the world and in our churches today. For pure and true prophets from the bible declares the nature, characters and how they perform what God instructed and directed them to do.

I want us to read some verses from the bible and understand more of what I am trying to reveal to you.

(2KINGS 9:1-13)

*AND ELISHA the prophet called one of the sons of the prophets and said to him, Gird up your hand, and go to Ramoth – gilead. When you arrive, look there for Jehu son of Jehoshaphat son of Nimshi; and go in and have him arise from among his brethren and lead him to an inner chamber. Then taken the cruse of oil and pour it on his head and say, Thus says the Lord: I have anointed you king over Israel. Then open the door and flee: do not tarry. So the young man, the young prophet, went to Ramoth – gilead. And when he came, the captains of the army were sitting outside; and he said, I have a message for you, O captain. Jehu said, To you, O captain. And Jehu arose, and they went into the house. And the prophet poured the oil on Jehu's head and said to him. Thus says the Lord, the God of Israel: I have anointed you king over the people of the Lord, even over Israel. You shall strike down the house of Ahab your master, that I may avenge the blood of My servants the prophets and of all the servants of the Lord [who have died] at the hands of Jezebel. For the whole house of Ahab shall perish, and I will cut off from Ahab every male, bond or free, in Israel. I will make the house of Ahab like the house of Jeroboam son of Nebat and like the house of Baasha son of Ahijah. [I Kings 21:22]. And the dogs shall eat Jezebel in the portion of Jezreel, and none shall bury her. And he opened the door and fled. When Jehu came out to the servants of his master, one said to him, Is all well? Why did this **mad fellow** come to you? And he said to them, you know that class of man and what he would say. And they said, that is false; tell us now. And he said, Thus and thus he spoke to me, saying, Thus says the Lord: I have anointed you king over Israel. Then they hastily took every man his garment and put it [for a cushion] under Jehu on the top of the [outside] stairs, and blew with trumpets, saying Jehu is kind!*

Now let us also look at another verse from the same chapter (2Kings 9:1-13).

People of God these is a very clear picture for us to know that even some prophets in the bible portrayed themselves like they were mad but they were not and even the life of **John The Baptist** gives us a perfect picture of their nature, character and features of prophets.

People of God it is good to be blessed by God and it is only God that makes a person rich but the devil (Satan) is also offering riches and wealth to prophets, men and women of God to enticed them and blind them for them to become his then later manipulate them to draw and attract souls to hell.

Believers, I personally know that the world or the universe was not created by the devil (Satan) but the pleasures and the anxieties of life in it are being generated by him. That is why Jesus Christ the light of the world refused and rejected the pleasure and the life anxieties of gaining wealth.

He knows that the things in it can be generated by the devil (Satan) but the universe itself is not for him so what sense will it make if you accept the devils offer and at the end you will die and leave all what you have gain through the devil in the universe without taking it with you when you die.

This is senseless if we are wise enough to understand what Jesus Christ meant when he refused and rejected the offer from the devil.

Precious one if you will agree with me on this one, what sense does it make to receive wealth and riches from the devil (Satan) in God's universe? The devil himself is under God and he was made by God, he gain all his senses of life by God - his nose to smell, eyes to see, mouth to talk, teeth to bite, tongue to taste all these things weren't created by him.

So you just imagine he is nothing before God, let's say; if God wants to take all these things from him what will he do. Therefore why will you or can you be deceived by a person or creature like this, until you yourself you are against God. Because if you receive anything from the devil, you will definitely die one day and you cannot take anything with you because the devil does not own the universe but God.

This is why the bible declares to us that "For *whoever wishes to save his life will lose it; but whoever loses his life for my sake will find it. 26"For what will it profit a man if he gains the whole world and forfeits his soul? Or what will a man give in exchange for his soul? 27"For the Son of Man is going to come in the glory of His Father with His angels and will then repay every man according to his deeds....*

(Matthew 16:26-27)

But we should rather seek God first and everything shall be added onto us.

"For the pagans run after all these things and your heavenly father knows you need them. But seek first his kingdom and his righteousness and all these things will be given to you as well"

(Matthew 6:32-33).

The bible even declares that *"for where your treasure is will be that's there your heart will be also".* (Matthew 6:21).

But the devils has blocked our ears and blind our eyes with wealth, pleasure in the world for us not to hear or see the truth and how the coming of the lord is near.

The devil has choked us with wealth and eagerness of getting rich so we can't preach the good news and we are not even aware that the coming of the lord is near.

In fact when was the last time you visited a church that they were preaching and the pastor or the prophet was talking about repentance, end times and helping the members to repent, taking them through the process of forgiveness teaching them to confess their sins and praying for them to receive the Holy Spirit Baptism.

Trust me brothers and sisters, all this good news about God and Jesus Christ is missing in so many churches of today, because most of the prophets, men and women of God are busy preaching success, prosperity, what to do and what not to do to gain riches and some are prophesying and declaring God's blessing on the souls; those who are not repented, unbelievers and pagans.

This is ridiculous because at the end of the day their souls are going to perish in hell to eternal destruction. May the lord have mercy and pity for our souls in his favour, grace and pleasure?

Because what is the benefit of prophecies on souls that has not repent, but first we should reveal to them about *repentance*, tell them the *end times* about the second coming of Christ Jesus to take repented souls with him to heaven.

But people have force themselves by the help and support of the devil to become false prophets and they are stealing killing and destroying blind and lost souls in the church today.

Precious one, in today's world prophecies are being sold for money which are false from false prophets. I know of a certain church on the internet that is asking people to call them for free prophetic word because they want to globalize the prophetic word. I am not going to write or mention names because I want you to analyze how people are using the name of God to prophecy to people but they are not true prophecies from God.

Please these are false; we should read the bible and the revelations from the bible which will speak to us because this is really getting out of hands. Though it is true that the lord God will do nothing, but he revealed his secrets unto his servants the prophets.

> "Surely the Lord GOD does nothing Unless He reveals His secret counsel To His servants the prophets."

(Amos 3:7).

But we shouldn't allow the devil to use his false prophet's, hide behind the scriptures from the bible to deceive us. God have prophets but we should also understand that we are all prophets because God speaks to everyone in a special way, God use dreams to speak to us, visions, trances and anything around us; Is just that we must be sensitive to the Holy Spirit when He is manifesting.

People of God, God love us and he doesn't want us to perish in hell so we should be careful of the lord's warnings to us concerning this end times.

Please we should study the bible very well for us not be deceived. Even if it's true that God does nothing until he revealed the secrets to his servants the prophets, please we must understand that we are all God's servants (prophets) and every servant of God is a prophet. That is what the bible means when it says servants the prophets not prophets his servants. This is because we are all servants of God and we are all serving the lord, therefore we are His prophets.

And I want you to believe me on this one, God has a very special way of speaking to every servant of his, some are through hearing the voice of God or the Holy Spirit, and some are through dreams, visions and trances.

In fact God respect us so he really speaks to us individually is just that at times we doubt whether is real or is from God or shall it come to pass.

Because people of God, secretes is shared between two people and if a third party should hear or one should heard of it, it doesn't become secrete any more.

Please this means the scripture is telling us that God have been revealing his secrets to us and we should be respectful of our dreams, visions and other ways God have been using to communicate to us.

People of God, I keep on saying or asking that why? Why is that Jesus Christ is telling us and warning us to be vigilant and careful of false prophets when the *end time* is coming because there will be a breed of them.

False prophets will be breeding all over the world and be deceiving many to their side.

Please with this Insight, foresight, greater, higher and deeper revelation about what the world or the church is getting into really defines that the world is coming into the end.

But what I keep asking and asking my self is are we preaching the good news. Now some one might ask what the good news is.

Good news is about the testimony of Jesus Christ, who came to die for our sins by sharing his blood on the cross through crucifixion and he died but on the third day rose up from death and told us to go to all over the world to **Preach** the **GOOD NEWS**, and baptized those that will believe.

Precious people, so now we know what is the good news; many of us who called ourselves the preachers of the *Good News* have deviate and still deviating from the preaching of the gospel and everything has turn and still turning into prophecies and prophetic word because we don't or find it difficult to understand the word *preach.*

Had it not been this powerful revelation God has showed or given me, I wouldn't have also know to understand the word *preach* and will not even bother or consider to figure out the meaning of the word "**PREACH**".

But when Jesus Christ was telling us to go and preach the good news all over the world; He really meant something about the word *preach* and not just *preach* the good news but we should go to all over this world to **preach, Repentance, End times** to the world for the people to gain **Atonement** by reconciling to God through **confessing** of their sins and after that we should help and pray for them to receive and accept the **Holy Spirit** and his baptism for them to be able to walk in righteousness and holiness.

Beloved, the purpose of writing this book is by the deeper, greater and higher revelation from the Holy Spirits but not to condemn prophets and prophecies but we should be much very careful of what God have entrust to us to do.

We should preach, yes! Preach the good news to all over the world and baptized those who believe.

But it's like; prophecy from various types of prophets in the world today is blinding us from the good news which we are supposed to preach to the world.

People of God the Endtime message is missing today in our churches. Prophets have taken over the church because of the fancy and entertainment prophecies, people personal data's which has nothing to do with Salvation.

They are just making money, luxury, wealth and turning this to some kind of Professional Business. But believe me on this one, *"A man run up to JESUS CHRIST and asked him "good teacher what must I do before I inherit the kingdom of God"* JESUS said to this man *"to obey the commandments in the Bible"* by giving out examples the man responded to Jesus, *"master with this commandment I have obey from infancy"* – then Jesus said to this rich man *"go and sell all what you have to earn and gain eternal life"*. The Bible said that the man's face turned down and felt bad because he had great wealth.

(Matthew 19:16-24)

Precious One, is this not marvelous of what we must do to gain eternal life, we must sell what we have to give to the poor because is very hard for a rich man to enter in the kingdom of God. Then why are our Prophets and men of God of today competing with riches, wealth, owning private jets, desperately running around of becoming too much successful, which is going to weigh them down. for the Bible declares that where your treasure is there will be your heart.

This is exactly what brought the wife of lot down because of her great wealth and riches her heart was still at Sodom & Gomorrah and this arouse the pride in her and she disobeyed God and at the end she turned into a pillar of salt.

We should be careful men and women of God, I am not saying we should allow poverty to over shadow us or drain in poverty but we should be aware of the true good news which God wants us to *preach*.

By preaching repentance, end time for the people to know *atonement* and lead them to *confess* their sins and be baptized in the *Holy Spirit*.

In today's church or in our world today, Holy Spirit Baptizm is missing in the church, no one is preaching repentance, endtimes, no one is teaching atonement which is the procedure of forgiveness for sinners to confess their sins and be baptized in the Holy Spirit to be able to walk with JESUS CHRIST in Holiness.

Everything on their programs in the church is prophecy, gain territories, claiming possessions, taking what the enemy has stolen.

Please these are all good but of what benefit are these to us or mean to us when we takes possession of all we want to take possessed of and after that we die and didn't have eternal life.

People are prophesying for money, I know and I know that you are also aware of that we are blinding souls from inheriting the kingdom of God.

Too much of everything is bad and we must be aware that the devil has learned all this strategies of prophecy from the true prophets and he is generating false prophets among us, to win and draw souls for himself.

I remember that a friend of mine told me a story he was involved in that, *"he was invited by a very great man of God to preach in his church and after the sermon he asked for normal service collection and he closed the congregation"*. He said to me that right after he closed the congregation the man of God who invited him called him and took him to his office and insulted him very well, the pastor said to my friend *"you are a very stupid man of God, foolish fool, village preacher. In fact where are you from and now that you have finished preaching, whose money do you want me to use to pay you"*. Then my friend said to me that on his next sermon at the same church he took money from the people in fact in a form of prophecies and consecrated seeds.

People of God we need revelation and the guidance, the direction of the Holy Spirit and the power of God to over come the enemy and we should be sensitive with his evil ways, we should test the Spirit to see if they are sent from God or not.

Precious one for example if you go to the market, grocery store or any super market to buy fruit or vegetables to come and eat in the house, do you just pick them up from the shop without checking whether it is rotten, expired or it doesn't smell till you buy and bring them home before you even eat them with your family?

Yes! Then why are we not applying the same process with these updated prophets with their delusion prophecies.

Believers, with me I feel it so strongly that many people are being deceived out there and I see it vividly how they are working. Please we should wake up from our sleep for the Endtime is already here.

Jesus Christ said we should preach the good news to all over the world not prophecy the good news to make luxury out of people.

He said we should preach which means we should *preach, repentance, Endtimes* and teach the people *Atonement* (which is the process of forgiveness – how they can be forgiven of their sins, iniquities). And this can only be done through *confession* of one's sins and after that we should baptized them with or in the *Holy Spirit*.

Brothers and Sisters this is what is required of us as men and women of God. Please we should not be blind by what the enemy is doing through fancy and entertainment prophecies.

We should go to places where we can hear and listen to the good news of God "what will shocked and surprised us, the endtimes that will be revealed to us for us to be revived of our sins, learn the process and procedure of how our sins can be Atone for, and by the revelation in this book we realized that this can only be done through confession, just confessing our sins with our mouth and we are liberated from the chains of our sins.

After that we seek how and what can help us not to go back to our sins again and get into deep and deeper relationship with God and Christ Jesus. Now we also realized that it's by or through the Holy Spirit that can guide us, be our comforter and our advocate but how can the Holy Spirit come to us, through or by being baptized by the Holy Spirit or with Holy Spirit.

> Believers trust me this is the only way you can be able to walk with God in his Holiness for the bible declares that we should *"Make every effort to live in peace with everyone and to be holy; without holiness no one will see the Lord"*.
>
> (Hebrews 12:14).

And I asked you how can you walk in Holiness or be holy whilst you have not been baptized with or by Holy Spirit.

Precious One, please continue to enjoy the deeper, higher and greater revelation in this book. Please pray and open your heart and spirit to be touched and know what's going on in the world today for the Endtime is already here.

CHAPTER TWO

REPENTANCE AND REVELATION

REPENTANCE

Repentance is a compound word that results in a complete transformation. It means "*to have a change of mind and heart*". The Apostle Paul put it this way, "Therefore, if anyone is in Christ, he is a new creation; old things have passed away; behold, all things have become new" **(2 COR. 5:17)**. *Therefore if any person is [ingrafted] in Christ (the Messiah) he is a new creation (a new creature altogether); the old [previous moral and spiritual condition] has passed away. Behold the fresh and new has come!*

When Jesus told Nicodemus, "You must repent". Nicodemus was a Pharisee, but he was not a believer. He was a member of the Sanhedrin, but he was not saved. He was rich by Jerusalem standards but poor by the standards of heaven.

Repentance implies you are heading in one direction and suddenly you turn and proceed in the opposite direction. It is an exchange of destinations. An unrepentant person is headed for hell. A repentant person has heaven as his or her final port of call. Repentance involves an exchange of authority. Before repentance you live under your own authority. After repentance you live under the authority of Christ. This is not a reformation but a rebirth.

Since the time of Adam and Eve from the beginning of creation, God have been calling his children to turn to him. I must say God has been telling and asking his children to repent so we might not be eternally destroyed. Sin has been one of the characteristics of mankind after creation but thanks be to God of his mercies that he has made it possible through his only be gotten son JESUS CHRIST for mankind to have a chance of repenting.

Repentance is expressing our sorrow of our sins acknowledging that we are lost believing in JESUS CHRIST and turning to God.

The greatest or the most relevant reason God sent his son Jesus Christ on earth to share his blood on the cross for mankind to gain salvation was because he want his children to repent.

Therefore I don't believe that if mankind request to repent from his sinful ways, God is going to let the blood of his son JESUS CHRIST sacrificed on the cross be meaningless.

God's greatest agenda is for his daughters and son's to repent and turn to him and gain salvation, apart from that I don't think there is nothing important to God. God wants us to regret from our sins so he can forgive us, he wants us to acknowledge the truth, gain a new heart and Spirit, escape from disaster and gain eternal life.

If this wasn't important or not necessary to God there is no way he would have let repentance be his theme and call all his people to repent.

I am saying repentance is the theme of God because from the Old Testament to the New Testament his main agenda is for his children to repent. That is why from the beginning of the bible he sends out his prophets and angels by carrying out repenting messages to his people, kingdoms, and nations.

God have been commanding his people to repent and I want us to depend on some of the scriptures from the bible to know the truth about what I am writing.

(JER 18:11)

> *"Now therefore say to the men of Judah and to the inhabitants of Jerusalem, Thus says the Lord: Behold, I am shaping evil against you and devising a plan against you. Return now each one from his evil way; reform now each one from his evil; reform your [accustomed] ways and make your [individual] actions good and right."*

(EZE 18:30-32)

> *"Therefore I will judge you, O house of Israel, every one according to his ways, says the Lord God. Repent and turn from all your transgressions, lest iniquity be your ruin and so shall they not be a stumbling block to you".*

(Acts. 17:30)

> *"Such [former] ages of ignorance God, it is true, ignored and allowed to pass unnoticed; but now He charges all people everywhere to repent (to heartily to amend their ways, with abhorrence of their past sins".*

(2PE 3:9)

> *"The Lord does not delay and is not tardy or slow about what He promises according to some people's conception of slowness, but He is long-suffering (extraordinarily patient) toward you, not desiring that any should perish, but that all should turn to repentance".*

As we can see from the scriptures above we can now totally believe that repentance has been the theme of God. Even the mission of JESUS CHRIST the son of God on earth was proclaiming the good news of God by preaching repentance "The times has come, the kingdom of God is near. Repent and believe the good news!"

(MARK 1:14 – 15)

Now after John was arrested and put in prison, Jesus came into Galilee, preaching the good news (the Gospel) of the kingdom of God. And saying, The [appointed period of] time is fulfilled (completed), and the kingdom of God is at hand; repent (have a change of mind which issues in regret for past sins and in change of conduct for the better) and believe (trust in, rely on, and adhere to) the good news (the Gospel).

Preaching repentance was the main factor, the main reason Jesus Christ came on earth. Besides Jesus Christ, preached the good news!!
and urged His disciples at that time with him to also carry out the good news to all over the world before he was taken up to heaven.

His disciples obediently but through difficulties carried out the good news till today from one generation to another. Now is our turn to carry on the mission of preaching repentance, End times, atonement confession and Holy Spirit baptism in the world or to the four corners of the earth.

(LUKE 24:46-48)

And said to them, Thus it is written that the Christ (the Messiah) should suffer and on the third day rise from (among) the dead, [Hos. 6:2.], and that repentance [with a view to and as the condition of] forgiveness of sins should be preached in His name to all nations, beginning from Jerusalem. You are witnesses of these things.

For this I would like and love to give out my knowledge about the essential aspects of repentance.

- Acknowledging we are lost
- Expressing sorrow for sin
- Returning to the father (God)
- Believing in Jesus Christ
- Doing good works

Precious one; writing this book is also a means of preaching to you or to the world. It doesn't have to be me standing on the pulpit before one can know that this is also a means of preaching. So I will recommend or urge you to be very serious about the deep things in this book.

Because after the creation of mankind repentance has been a command from God to mankind therefore repentance is a very serious task and an important factor for mankind to achieve because God has plan a severe disaster for those that refuse to repent. But because God doesn't want his children to suffer eternal destruction he has made it possible for mankind to gain repentance through the blood of his son Jesus Christ.

Let me take the opportunity to hint on the good reasons why mankind need to gain or achieve repentance.

- Escape from disaster
- Forgiveness of your sins
- A new heart and spirit
- A knowledge of the truth
- Salvation
- Eternal life

My brothers and sisters, I am still telling you to repent if you haven't because of what I have seen and heard from the revelation given to me by God through the inspiration of the Holy Spirit. For the bible declares that, *"the death of the unrighteous is very detestable to God."*

Precious one, the above scripture should let us be afraid, frightened and fear the word of God because he is God and he does what pleases him. Repentance is very important to God that's why out of a sacrificial love he sacrificed his only begotten son to use his blood to cleanse our sins.

By this God have made a covenant with the blood of his son Jesus Christ that anyone who regret and repent of his or her sins and turn back to him, He is an honest and just God that he will forgive you and clean you from your sins by the blood of Jesus Christ and your sins shall be remembered no more.

Believers all you need is to forget about your pride, acknowledge that you are lost, express sorrow for your sins return to God and believe in Jesus Christ.

In fact God is good, and the Holy Spirit is working well. This draws my mind to one of the disciple of Jesus Christ in the Bible called Peter. You know I will say or describe Peter as the leader or one of the leaders of Jesus Christ twelve (12) disciples which I always called them *the twelve disciplines* because they followed Jesus Christ to be disciplined, they learned and studied Jesus Christ.

In fact I can say they were schooled by Jesus Christ. I used the world disciplined because after they became the disciples of Jesus Christ their way of living changed in the sense that, the way they walk, talk, dress eat and even the way they were doing their business changed.

But of what I want to say about Peter is very interesting and powerful. Peter was the first disciple Christ Jesus called and this made him the leader and closer to Jesus Christ, he was sent to anywhere; and everywhere Jesus Christ will go he will never be absent.

In fact he was a true friend of Jesus Christ even to the limit or the point of telling Jesus Christ that he will die with him and promise to go to anywhere with him even to the point of death.

Could you ever remember that it was this same peter that was bold to walk on water to get closer to Jesus Christ? Peter was the brave one among the disciples. But Peter, people of God after all the love, interesting experience and the enjoyment he shared with Jesus Christ, he denied Jesus Christ three (3) good times when it was at the point of Jesus Christ death.

> "Now Peter was sitting out in the courtyard, and a servant girl came to him. "You also were with Jesus of Galilee," she said.
>
> 70 But he denied it before them all. "I don't know what you're talking about," he said.

71 Then he went out to the gateway, where another servant girl saw him and said to the people there, "This fellow was with Jesus of Nazareth."

72 He denied it again, with an oath: "I don't know the man!"

73 After a little while, those standing there went up to Peter and said, "Surely you are one of them; your accent gives you away."

74 Then he began to call down curses, and he swore to them, "I don't know the man!"

Immediately a rooster crowed. 75 Then Peter remembered the word Jesus had spoken: "Before the rooster crows, you will disown me three times." And he went outside and wept bitterly

(Matthew 26:69:75)

Father I thank you for your sweet revelation, In fact I am happy yet not happy of what peter did to Jesus Christ but I am very happy of what happen after he denied, betrayed, and disappointed Jesus Christ.

The Bible declares that after Peter disappointed, betrayed and denied Jesus Christ he regretted, cried, felt sorrow of his sins, he acknowledged that he has done wrong and he repented of his sins.

And precious one reading this book do you know what happened after Jesus Christ resurrected from his death. He mandated and reinstated Peter to greatness; he made Peter the rock upon which he will build his church.

Aren't you happy my friend, after all the disappointment, betrayals, denials, fornications, adultery, drunkenness and even your curses of sins that are detestable to God? God is still using this revelation to speak to you that, it doesn't matter how great are your sins, it doesn't matter what you did yesterday, today and even your willful sins, God will still and can still forgive you and make you his son or daughter again, even mandate you for greatness because of the blood of his son Jesus Christ sacrificed on the cross.

Tell me, what you will do if someone betray, disappoint and denies you like how Peter did to Jesus Christ. But this is to tell us that, for this reason are what makes God the almighty God, king of kings and lord of lords.

Come on! Be free from anything that is binding you up, any chains of sins that is making you stagnant in your life; and that curse sin of pride that is preventing and stopping you from acknowledging that you are lost.

Return to God and believe in Jesus Christ because is by and through his blood that we have this chance and opportunity of salvation. I urge you to begin to do good, pray for a new heart and spirit, seek the truth and gain eternal life. People of God, repent and May the lord helps you to repent; because regret without repentance will lead you to death.

May we look at another powerful story of repentance seen in the bible in the book of...?

(Luke 7:36-50)

"*When one of the Pharisees invited Jesus to have dinner with him, he went to the Pharisee's house and reclined at the table. [37] A woman in that town who lived a sinful life learned that Jesus was eating at the Pharisee's house, so she came there with an alabaster jar of perfume. [38] As she stood behind him at his feet weeping, she began to wet his feet with her tears. Then she wiped them with her hair, kissed them and poured perfume on them.*

[39] When the Pharisee who had invited him saw this, he said to himself, "If this man were a prophet, he would know who is touching him and what kind of woman she is—that she is a sinner."

[40] Jesus answered him, "Simon, I have something to tell you."

"Tell me, teacher," he said.

[41] "Two people owed money to a certain moneylender. One owed him five hundred denarii,[a] and the other fifty.

⁴² Neither of them had the money to pay him back, so he forgave the debts of both. Now which of them will love him more?"

⁴³ Simon replied, "I suppose the one who had the bigger debt forgiven."

"You have judged correctly," Jesus said.

⁴⁴ Then he turned toward the woman and said to Simon, "Do you see this woman? I came into your house. You did not give me any water for my feet, but she wet my feet with her tears and wiped them with her hair. ⁴⁵ You did not give me a kiss, but this woman, from the time I entered, has not stopped kissing my feet. ⁴⁶ You did not put oil on my head, but she has poured perfume on my feet. ⁴⁷ Therefore, I tell you, her many sins have been forgiven— as her great love has shown. But whoever has been forgiven little loves little."

⁴⁸ Then Jesus said to her, "Your sins are forgiven."

⁴⁹ The other guests began to say among themselves, "Who is this who even forgives sins? "Jesus said to the woman, "Your faith has saved you; go in peace."

Precious one, as we read for ourselves in the above scripture, the bible depicts of a woman who was caught fornicating in public and they brought her to Jesus Christ to condemn her but when she was brought to Jesus Christ, very astonishing to those that brought her. Instead of Jesus Christ to condemn her to destruction so they can get the chance to stone her to death, Jesus Christ bend down to write on the ground for a few minutes but no one knew what he was writing or what he wrote, he lifted his head to the people that caught and brought the woman to him and he said to them *"if anyone who is without sin should be the first to stone this woman"*. Then all of them was quiet and Jesus bend down to write on the ground again yet still no one knew what he was writing or what he wrote but before He lifted up his head to speak to the people for the second time no one was there, all of them has departed.

Jesus then said to the woman whose name was not even mention in the bible that "*woman your sins have been forgiven therefore you are free go and sin no more*". Precious one isn't this also great, how a long time prostitute has just been forgiven of all her heavy burden of sins because the punishment of her sins was to be stone to death which would have been a very heavy death.

I am just very happy of this chance and an everlasting opportunity from Jesus Christ; let's just imagine if Jesus Christ wasn't in the picture what would have happened to this woman. The existence of Jesus Christ gave this prostitute woman the opportunity or a very powerful chance to escape disaster, isn't this awesome!

Friends, the story of this woman didn't just end there when Jesus Christ told her to go; for her sins have been forgiven. The bible then declared that this woman regretted of her sins and cried around in search of Jesus Christ weeping from house to house and later she was told that Jesus Christ was in a rich man's called *Simon the leper's* house.

Beloved by reading it from the scriptures to find the truth, we realized that when the woman whose sins have been forgiven noticed that Jesus was in Simon the leper's house, she rushed quickly to where Jesus was and when she found Jesus there she burst in tears out of bitterness and used her tears to wash the feet of Jesus, used her hair to cleaned it and later used an expensive perfume which I will say the most expensive perform (fragrance) of that time to anoint the feet of Jesus Christ.

Precious one, don't you feel the power in this revelation, but I know the question that is going through your mind and is what is also running through my mind. My problem is; first of all, why and how should Jesus Christ allow a prostitute to anoint his feet. And even with that; where and how this woman did got the money to buy this expensive perfume because when the disciples saw the perfume, they confirmed that the perfume is very expensive and even a year's wages cannot be enough to buy that perfume.

On a serious note, why did this woman use her tears to wash Jesus Christ feet, use her hair to clean them and never stopped kissing the feet of Jesus Christ.

Do you know that the bible declares that the glory of a woman is her hair but this woman uses her glory to wipe the feet of Jesus Christ? People of God if this woman was from a rich or a reputable home there is no way she would have prostituted and even if she would indulge in prostitution she wouldn't have done it in public because of her reputation and dignity or for the respect of her family or home. But I believe this woman was very poor, from a poor home and no one misses or cares about her so she is not treated with respect; people sleep with her in public for money before she can get money to feed herself, buy clothing's to wear and even get a place to sleep. And due to her situation if she have had a place of her own there is no way she would have been prostituting in public, she would have taken the men to her house to cover up her disgrace but this woman was a public prostitute because she has no home or place to lay her head or sleep.

Precious one, I would like you to tap into your thoughts and follow this revelation carefully, because with such a low class prostitute where did she have the money to buy such expensive perfume to anoint the feet of Jesus Christ. Beloved, I believe she gathered the money through prostitution to be able to anoint the feet of Jesus Christ.

Now I want you to understand something from the scripture (Matthew 26:6-13), *Now when Jesus came back to Bethany and was in the house of Simon the leper, A woman came up to Him with an alabaster flask of very precious perfume, and she poured it on His head as He reclined at table. And when the disciples saw it, they were indignant, saying, For what purpose is all this waste? For this perfume might have been sold for a large sum and the money given to the poor. But Jesus, filly aware of this, said to them, Why do you bother the woman? She has done a noble (praise-worthy and beautiful) thing to Me. For you always have the poor among you, but you will not always have Me. [Deut, 15:11.] In pouring this perfume on My body she has done something to prepare Me for My burial. Truly I tell you, wherever this good news (the Gospel) is preached in the whole world, what this woman has done will be told also, in memory of her.*

After this woman have use this expensive perfume (fragrance) to anoint the feet of Jesus Christ, the disciples around even the rich man (Simon) were talking and murmuring against what the woman have done.

But Jesus Christ shouted them up and said to them not to bother the woman because what she has done is good *"when she poured this perfume on my body she did it to prepare me for burial. I tell you the truth, wherever this gospel is preached throughout the world, what she has done will also be told in memory of her"*.

Isn't this magnificent, because of repentance a low class prostitute has been in history from that day till today and even to the end of the world, which makes her now a great person. But to tell the truth I will say this woman is really the definition of repentance.

Precious one is there any way you could bear with me that when Jesus Christ was looking for someone to prepare him for burial, a prostitute was chosen and when he was looking for someone to build his church on, he chose Peter who betrayed, denied and disappointed him at the time that he needed him most.

My brothers and sisters I am not writing or revealing to you to continue with your sins but rather convicting you to acknowledge that you are lost, feel sorrow and regret for your sins, turn back to God and believe in Jesus Christ. Because all that you might be going through or been through might be a process of your greatness, don't let noting stop you or pride prevent you from humbling yourself now, begin to speak to your sins that enough is enough.

Many people in the bible or from the bible were sinners or got involve in great sins but at the end they regretted and repented. And all that they were involved in was a contribution to their greatness.

You just imagine if this woman shouldn't have been through prostitution would she have been great, would she have been imparted so much to gain salvation. Precious one this is your chance and a very great opportunity for you to be saved. Please repent, begin to pray yourself out of this heavy burden of sin, breakout of those chains of iniquities, come out of that darkness and acknowledge the truth which is the light of the world.

Turn back to God, believe in Jesus Christ and be exposed to rightness and holiness. The woman prostitute felt she was free from a heavy burden of sins that was why she cried and was very appreciative to what Jesus Christ has done for her. Please be free kindly help yourself out to be free from your sins. I need you to repent right now because the end results of those who don't repent is death.

<u>REVELATION</u>

People of God, the disclosure of God and his truth have been the Unsearchable thing for mankind to comprehend and a difficult task for mankind from the beginning of the world to disclose. But by the help of his Holy Spirit, revelation is revealing God and his truth to His people (children). And revealing God to someone who doesn't know God or don't believe in God is trying to preach or teach repentance to the person to accept Jesus Christ the son of God as his or her personal savior.

Therefore I could say that revelation of God or from God makes one repent from his or her sins and infirmities because it helps you know the deeper and greater things of how sovereign the lord is; and how impossible to understand God but out of the impossible we find or get possible things to understand about God but this is because the day that mankind get to know or totally understand God almighty; then I believe everything of God or about God becomes meaningless to us which will make mankind decide not to seek after God anymore. Because you will now know what is of Him; how he works, does his things and he become common to you then after all what is there to search for or about God again?

This is the reason God has let mankind be a searching tool to search and seek after God to know more of Him and His truth.

From the beginning of the world till now mankind or no one under the planet has been able to discover who God is; where He comes from or How He became God. But whether to find out or not to find out; He is God and by Him you and I were created and formed including the universe that we dwell in. Therefore all we need to do is to obey Him, believe Him and accept whatever He wants us to accept, He is God and we can't use the mind that He has given us to think of Him to challenge Him; because He is the maker of our mind and has the power to operate our mind any how he pleases.

He is God and He gave us the eyes to see, nose to breath, mouth to talk, ears to hear, voice to be heard and I will say all of the senses and elements of humanities besides He has built a powerful universe for mankind to dwell in. This is good, powerful and these make him God. until mankind can provide for himself or herself nose to breath, eyes to see, mouth to talk, tongue to taste, ears to hear and also create or design his or her own universe to dwell in or stay in, then mankind can think of challenging God or dispute the fact that God is God.

And if God is God then we must believe, understand and accepts everything that He wants us to believe understands and accept. But not asking God questions and why we should obey Him or what He wants us to believe, accept and understand. Believers God is God and doesn't own anybody an explanation about how and why He is God. Whether we understand or not it is through Him that we are here in existence, we are under and made by his supernatural powers.

Therefore God in his kindness and love for his children has made it possible for mankind to be able to disclose God and his truth through revelation or through the inspiration of his Holy Spirit. This means through the inspiration of the Holy Spirit, revelation of God or about God are being revealed to mankind to know and understand God in his own way.

Even through the same revelation we understand that the Holy Bible was written by men through the inspiration of the Holy Spirit. The men who wrote the bible were inspired by the Holy Spirit to be able to write the bible.

Because from the beginning of the Bible to the end of it, we were not witnesses of the incident that happened in the Bible but by the powerful revelation of God and through the inspiration of his Holy Spirit we are able to believe, understand and accept everything from the bible.

Precious One God is powerful, He is a supernatural God, Omnipotent, Omniscient, Omnipresent and he is almighty. Before him there was no God and after Him there is no God coming. God is the only one who has the power to prove to you that he is powerful.

The Bible declares that God is a Spirit and no one have seen him and no one can see him and because he is a Spirit therefore we must worship serve him in Spirit and in truth.

> *"Yet a time is coming and has now come when the true worshipers will worship the father in spirit and truth, for they are the kind of worshippers the father seeks. God is spirit and his worshippers must worship in spirit and in truth."*

(John 4:23-24).

But because God wants to have close, personal and emotional relationship with mankind, He has then make Himself known to mankind by manifesting Himself visibly through His only begotten son Jesus Christ, King of Kings. I have known that this revelation will be difficult for anyone who does not already know God and understand His Supernatural works to believe. Because I have encounter difficult times explaining this revelation to people over and over again.

Anytime I try to preach God and repentance to people, they will be like they are okay but as soon as you reveal His Son Jesus Christ; you create confusion in their mind and their thoughts.

Many people keep asking me that *"with God they believe He is God but their problem is; His son JESUS CHRIST"*.

And their problem is how Jesus Christ did became the son of God and how was He born, if reality birth is between a man and a woman but with JESUS CHRIST it wasn't like that, then how was it possible.

In fact I myself have had difficult and a very hard times to explain this again and again to people because the revelation in this message is supernatural, it's beyond the thought of mankind.

But the bible which has been our source of answer to every question we need to ask God, declares that in the beginning was the *word*, and the *word* was with God and the *word* was God. He was with God in the beginning and through Him what was made has been made. In him was life and that life was the light of men the light shows in darkness but the darkness has not understood it.

(JOHN 1:1-5-16)

And the Light shines on in the darkness, for the darkness has never overpowered it [put it out or absorbed it or appropriated it, and is unreceptive to it]. There came a man sent from God, whose name was John. [Mal. 3:1.] This man came to witness, that he might believe in it [adhere to it, trust it, and rely upon it] through him. He was not the Light himself, but came that he might bear witness regarding the Light. There it was – the true Light [was then] coming into the world [the genuine, mperfect, steadfact Light] ·that illumines every person. [Isa. 49:6.]. He came into the world, and though the world was made through Him, the world did not recognize Him [did not know Him]. He came to that which belonged to Him [to His own – His domain, creation, things, would], and they who were His own did not receive Him and did not welcome Him. But to as many as did receive and welcome in, He gave the authority (power, privilege, right) to become the children of God, that is, to those who believe in (adhere to, trust in, and rely on) His name – [Isa. 56:5]. Who owe their birth neither to bloods nor to the flesh [that of physical impulse] nor to the will of man [that of a natural father], but to God. [They are born of God!]. And the Word (Christ) became flesh (human, incarnate) and tabernacle (fixed His tent of flesh, lived awhile) among us; and we [actually] saw His glory (His honor, His majesty), such glory as an only begotten son receives from his father, full of grace (favor, loving – kindness) and truth. [Isa. 40:5]. John testified about Him and cried out, This was He of Whom I said, He Who comes after me has priority over me, for He was before me. [He takes rank above me, for He existed before I did. He has advanced before me, because He is my Chief.] For out of His fullness (abundance0 we have all received [all had a share and we were all supplied with] one grace after another and spiritual blessing upon spiritual blessing and even favor upon favor and gift [heaped] upon gift.

Brothers and Sisters reading this book, for those who believe I praise God but to those who find it difficult to believe and understand the revelation about who and how Jesus Christ came into the picture or to existence, I pray that the Holy Spirit Himself should inspires you to understand this more and better.

Precious One, by the inspiration of the Holy Spirit we understand that "the word was God" and the word became flesh and made his dwelling among us. Please I would love you to read through the above bible verse patiently to understand and be inspired more. And if you still don't understand how the word became flesh, i would love to use this opportunity to remember you from the Bible that the "***word***" was spoken to a virgin called Mary by an angel sent from God. And the bible declares that the Holy Spirit came upon the virgin and the power of God over shadowed the virgin and she became pregnant by the word though the supernatural power of God and the virgin gave birth to the word and the word became flesh.

"In the sixth month of Elizabeth's pregnancy, God sent the angel Gabriel to Nazareth, a town in Galilee, ²⁷ to a virgin pledged to be married to a man named Joseph, a descendant of David. The virgin's name was Mary. ²⁸ The angel went to her and said, "Greetings, you who are highly favoured! The Lord is with you."

²⁹ Mary was greatly troubled at his words and wondered what kind of greeting this might be. ³⁰ But the angel said to her, "Do not be afraid, Mary; you have found favour with God. ³¹ You will conceive and give birth to a son, and you are to call him Jesus. ³² He will be great and will be called the Son of the Most High. The Lord God will give him the throne of his father David, ^{33} *and he will reign over Jacob's descendants forever; his kingdom will never end."*

^{34} *"How will this be," Mary asked the angel, "since I am a virgin?"*

^{35} *The angel answered, "The Holy Spirit will come on you, and the power of the Most High will overshadow you. So the holy one to be born will be called*[a] *the Son of God.* ^{36} *Even Elizabeth your relative is going to have a child in her old age, and she who was said to be unable to conceive is in her sixth month.* ^{37} *For no word from God will ever fail."*

^{38} *"I am the Lord's servant," Mary answered. "May your word to me be fulfilled?" Then the angel left her."*

(Luke 1:26-38).

People of God, like I said from the beginning God is God and He owes know one explanation about His supernatural powers, How He performs and operates at the end of it all, He is still God and we are all also made by His supernatural powers therefore why won't we obey Him, follow His commands, belief, accepts and understands whatever he wants us to understands. It does not matter for me to ask Him why but it does matter for me to be obedient to him and never challenge Him because He made me and how I was even formed and created out of my mother's womb I have no Idea but all I know is I am here in his universe and I am enjoying His glory.

The Bible also makes us understand that the word didn't just become flesh for no reason but the word became flesh for a purpose which is because of this purpose we have been saved and achieved eternal salvation.

JESUS CHRIST who was and is the word of God was born through the Virgin Mary to save the world and cleans mankind from the abominable act by Adam and Eve which was disobeying and breaking the loyalty between God and mankind. Therefore is the blood of Jesus Christ that was used as a sacrifice to nullify, sanctify, edify and fortify mankind spirit, soul and body for us to be able to inherit and enjoy eternal salvation in the kingdom of God.

From the above story was the reason JESUS CHRIST came to earth through the manner of GODS word becoming the Holy Seed in the womb of a virgin and the word become flesh and Jesus Christ was bring forth.

Beloved He was born as we too were born from the womb of our mothers, so He was also human, with all the human senses of humanities.

The Bible declared that he grew as a normal human being, stronger, found favor from men and from God.

> *"And Jesus grew in wisdom and stature and in favor with God and men".*

(Luke 2:52)

Based on His purpose to bring salvation to mankind in the world, He loved the things of God, listened to the word of God and asked question and gave answers about God.

Gradually Jesus Christ grew in wisdom, become more influenced with his relationship with God and got too much addicted to the things of God also to be able to fulfill His purpose on earth and accomplish the will of His father – God. Jesus Christ left home to fast and prays for forty days and forty nights at where the spirit of God led Him.

The Bible explained to us that after His fasting and prayers for forty days and forty nights the spirit of God led Him into the desert and there He was tempted by the devil.

But by the power of God which is upon Him, overcame the devil; and the devil run away from Jesus Christ.

Beloved going through the Bible to understand more of what the Holy Spirit is revealing to us we realized that Jesus Christ the son of the living God wasn't obsessed with pleasures of the world, worldly gains and material stuffs so the devil couldn't over powered Him.

Because the devil (Satan) tried to offer Jesus Christ the world and everything in it including the money, cars, wealth, luxury, riches, women and mansions But Jesus Christ with the knowledge that all those things are vanity, materialistic and it will not last forever and everything shall pass away except the word of God, He rejected them and never bows to the devil (Satan).

Precious One, unlike many prophets, men and women of God today, many of them have been able to accept the offer from the devil (Satan) and exchange the souls and their purpose on earth to enjoy the wealth, riches and the luxurious life from the devil (Satan) which will soon fade away when the time is right.

Many Prophet, Men and women of God today have been blind by the enemy (Lucifer) with these worldly pleasures and they are working falsely against God and his Kingdom.

But may I used this opportunity to advice my fellow prophets, men and women of God out there that if you are reading this book repent before Jesus Christ comes to meet you in your sins.

Beloved to continue with the inspiration of Jesus Christ, the Bible declares that after the devil was defeated by tempting him, He begun to preach repentance, the End times which is how the world is going to come to an end, therefore everyone must gain atonement (the procedure of forgiveness), how and what to do for God to forgive us our sins and He made the people believe that this can only be done by confession (which is confessing our sins to God and asking God to forgive us all our sins). And after that we should be baptized and gain Holy Spirit and walk or live a life of Holiness.

Brothers and Sisters, this is exactly what God wants us to preach to the world, His good news which is to understand the word preach and preach it to the people. Because the word preach carries the good news in it and God wanting us to preach; He wants us to preach the elements and the components of the word preach.

I know this must be a little bit confusion but by the inspiration of the Holy Spirit what I mean is; The word preach carries a message in the word itself and by the revelation giving to me by the Holy Spirit. The word preach means Preach, Repentance (Revelation), End times, Atonement, Confession and Holy Spirit (Baptism).

My fellow friends this is exactly what God want us to preach and win souls for his Kingdom. Isn't this revelation powerful, in fact I was short with words when I had this revelation and couldn't eat nor sleep for days because it is so powerful and it takes only the revelation giving to you by God to figure out what the word **"PREACH"** means.

Therefore now that we know and understand what God truly wants us to PREACH I believe we are all victims of preaching exactly what the Lord wants us to Preach and teach the people all over the world?

In addition, what we need to understand from this powerful   .
revelation is that, there is no way one can accept or receive the *Holy Spirit* and his Baptism until, he or she *confess* his or her sins to God and one cannot just confess his or her sins until he or she knows *atonement* the procedure of forgiveness which helps a person to confess his or her sins to be forgiven by God.

Also one cannot gain atonement or accept the procedure of forgiveness or feel that he or she have sin against God until repentance have been preach to him or her before he or she agrees to turn to God for forgiveness.

Believers these perfectly explains how we should preach the word to people all over the world to win and snatch souls for God but not vice versa by prophesying to the people, preaching and teaching success, riches, Gods wealth and prosperity to the people whilst they knew nothing about repentance, end times, atonement (procedure of forgiveness), confessing of their sins and receiving the Holy Spirit to be able to walk in righteousness and Holiness.

Firstly, we should preach repentance because when JESUS CHRIST begun preaching. This is what he preached to the people, about repentance for this kingdom of God is near.

Beloved, JESUS CHRIST really preached repentance to the people, draw the attention of many; win and snatch many souls to himself and thought them End time, atonement, confession and baptism (Holy Spirit).

And out of these He selected twelve disciples to be His followers, also trained them and schooled them to carry the message across the world.

Now for our physical and spiritual sins to be atoned for, forgiven and cleansed, Jesus Christ was crucified on the cross for His blood to be used to wiped away sin and iniquities also to renew and restore the loyalty between mankind and God which was broke by Adam and Eve when they disobey God and ate from the tree of life, good and evil.

Since we are all aware of the death and resurrection of Jesus Christ from the Bible and by the explanations through the Holy Spirit, we all believe and accept how true and real Jesus Christ is. But the most important of it all is when he was been taken to Heaven in the presence of this disciples, He ushered them to go into all over the world to preach the good news.

Beloved, this message is not for only his disciples present at that time but is a powerful message for us all to go ahead and proclaim the good news to all over the world.

Now the revelation about preaching the good news or to preach the good news makes the task very interesting and simple. To preach exactly what He expect of us to preach and miracles, signs and wonders will follow but not deviating over preaching to something else or prophetic and prophecies to make money, wealth fame and luxuries out of the poor.

I know it takes only the insight of God to know exactly what the word "PREACH" means and what Jesus Christ is expecting of us when He wanted and needed us to preach his good news to all over the world. But by the revelation through the inspiration of the Holy Spirit we are been made aware of the word preach, which means we should go to all over the world and Preach, Repentance, End times, Atonement, Confession and the Baptism of the Holy Spirit. This truly gives us a clear understanding and a powerful way to preach the good news and win souls for JESUS CHRIST.

I believe at this point, this powerful revelation is blowing your mind but I declare to you that don't be carried away for there are more revelation in this book to the end and powerful future prophecies Hidden in it.

Coming to think of it the revelation of the entire picture draws my mind to the last chapter of the Holy Bible which is *'revelation'* and in that chapter God revealed how the end time of this world will be through the Apostle John during his days on the Island of Patmos.

Beloved, if revelation means revealing some things about the past, present and future and the last chapter of the Holy Bible speaks of revelation of the past, present and future then that means there is or there will be more deeper, greater and higher things which God is revealing to us in the book of *revelation*. And I believe if we pay attention to be inspired by the Holy Spirit, the Holy Spirit will explain more of this chapter of the Bible *'Revelation'* to us.

But most at times, believers or Christians finds it more difficult to read and understand the last chapter of the Bible *'Revelation'* because it scares them and frightened them of how the world will end; the tribulations and the persecutions part of it. But I believe this is the strongest and powerful part of the Bible that provokes everyone who reads the book of *revelation* in the Bible to repent. Because no one wants to be left behind to be troubled by the Anti-Christ also to bear his mark (666) and suffer eternal destruction in Hell.

That is why I said earlier that preaching revelation of God to someone is revealing God and His truth to the person and this is totally preaching repentance to the person, because if someone doesn't know or believe God that means the person has not repent and he or she needs repentance to take or accept Jesus Christ the son of God as His lord and master savior.

Precious One, even the book of *revelation* is now being refused to preach in churches because everyone is preaching prosperity, success, Prophetic keys, making prophetic decrees and everybody wants to be a prophet and prophecy, all in the name of fame and wealth but the meaning of the good news is not being preached any more.

This makes it difficult for people or to see people living Holy life's, speaking in tongues, accepting and believing in the Holy Spirit and his baptism. Now people bares tattoo's on their skin or go for tattoos and even wears chains or anklets on their ankles and still feels comfortable in church because the preacher is not preaching the truth which is the good news of repentance but rather prophesying for fame and wealth also teaching how to be rich, successful and prosperous.

But Precious One, I believe preaching repentance and revealing the End times to them will convict them to seek atonement - the procedure of forgiveness which will enable them to confess their sins and believe to accept the baptism of the Holy Spirit to live a righteous and holy life's.

But in today's world is all about, Prophets and their different diversities of prophecies to gain fame and wealth. But may the lord touch your heart and open your eyes and mind to see and understand what the Holy Spirit is trying to reveal to you as you read this book, which speaks to us of what revelation has happened, what is happening and what is going to happen in the world that we are living in; the lord has been good to me to reveal deep things and greater things to me through the inspirations of the Holy Spirit. writing this book has made me love the last chapter 'Revelation' in the Bible because God have open my eyes and mind to see, read and understand the chapter in a very different way.

Beloved; Revelation is a very powerful chapter in the bible and I will recommend each and every one reading this book to also read 'revelation' the last chapter of the Bible.

In this last chapter of the Bible revelation reveals and explained to us how beautiful Heaven is, how awesome, glorious and powerful God is described, how true Jesus Christ is the son of God.

(REV. 4:1-11)

AFTER THIS I looked, and behold, a door standing open in heaven! And the first voice which I had heard addressing me like [the calling of] a war trumpet said, Come up here, and I will show you what must take place in the future. ²At once I came under the [Holy] Spirit's power, and behold, a throne stood in heaven, with one seated on the throne! [Ezek. 1:26]. ³And He Who sat there appeared like [the crystalline brightness of] jasper and [the fiery] sardius, and encircling the throne there was a halo that looked like [a rainbow of] emerald. [Ezek. 1:28.] ⁴Twently – four other thrones surrounded the throne, and seated on these thrones were twenty – four elders (the members of the heavenly Sanhedrin), arrayed in white clothing, with crowns of gold upon their heads. ⁵Out from the throne came flashes of lightning and rumblings and peals of thunder, and in front of the throne seven blazing torches burned which are the seven Spirits of God [the sevenfold Holy Spirit]; ⁶And in from of the throne there was also what looked like a transparent glassy sea, as if of crystal, And around the throne, in the center at each side of the throne, in the center at each side of the throne, were four living creatures (ones, beings) who were full of eyes in front and behind [with intelligence as to what is before and at the rear of them]. [Ezek. 1:5,18]. ⁷The first living creature (one, being) was like a lion, the second living creature like an ox, the third living creature had the face of a men, and the fourth living creature [was] like a flying eagle. [Ezek. 1:10.] ⁸And the four living creatures, individually having six wings, were full of eyes all over and within [underneath their wings]; and day and night they never stop saying, Holy, holy, holy is the Lord God Almighty (Omnipotent), who was and who is and who is to come. ⁹And whenever the living creatures offer glory and honor and thanksgiving to Him Who sits on the throne, who lives forever and ever (through the eternities of the eternities), [Ps. 47:8-1]. ¹⁰The twenty – four elders (the members of the heavenly Sanhedrin) fall prostrate before Him Who is sitting on the throne, and they worship Him Who lives forever and ever; and they throw down their crowns before the throw, crying out. ¹¹Worthy are you, our Lord and God, to receive the glory and the honor and dominion, for you created all things; by your will they were [brought into being] and were created [Ps. 19:1]

(REV. 5:1-14)

AND I saw lying on the open hand of Him Who was seated on the throne a scroll (book) written within and on the back, closed and sealed with seven seals; [Isa. 29:11; Ezek. 2:9, 10; Dan. 12:4] ²And I saw a strong angel announcing in a loud voice, Who is worthy to open the scroll? And [who is entitled and deserves and is morally fit] to break its seals? ³And no one in heaven or on earth or under the earth [in the realm of the dead, Hades] was able to open the scroll or to take a [single] look at its contents. ⁴And I wept audibly and bitterly because no one was found fit to open the scroll or to inspect it. ⁵Then one of the elders [of the heavenly Sanhedrin] said to me, Stop weeping! See, the Lion of the tribe of Judah, the Root (Source) of David, has won (has overcome and conquered)! He can open the scroll and break its seven seals! [Gen. 49:9, 10: Isa. 11:1, 10.] ⁶And there between the throne and the four living creatures (ones, beings) and among the elders [of the heavenly Sanhedrin] I saw a Lamb standing, as though it had been slain, with seven horns and with seven eyes, which are the seven Spirits of God [the sevenfold Holy Spirit] Who have been sent [on duty far and wide] into all the earth. [Isa. 53:7, Zech. 3:8, 9; 4:10.]. ⁷He then went and took the scroll from the right hand of Him Who sat on the throne. ⁸And when He had taken the scroll (book), the four living creatures and the twenty – four elders [of the heavenly Sanhedrin] prostrated themselves before the Lamb. Each was holding a harp (lute or guitar), and they had golden bowls full of incense (fragrant spices and gums for burning), which are the prayers of God's people (the saints). ⁹And [now] they sing a new song, saying, You are worthy to take the scroll and to break the seals that are on it, for You were slain (sacrificed), and with Your blood You purchased men unto God from every tribe and language and people and nation. [Ps. 33:3.]. ¹⁰And you have made them a kingdom (royal race) and priests to our God, and they shall reign [as Kings] over the earth! [Exod. 19:6; Isa. 61:6.]. ¹¹Then I looked, and I heard the voices of many angels on every side of the throne and of the living creatures and the elders [of the heavenly Sanhedrin], and they numbered ten thousand times ten

thousand and thousands of thousands, [Dan. 7:10]. *[12]Saying
in a loud voice, Deserving is the Lamb, Who was sacrificed,
to receive all the power and riches and wisdom and might
and honor and majesty (glory, splender) and blessing![13]And I
heard every created thing in heaven and on earth and under
the earth [in Hades, the place of departed spirits] and on
the sea and all that is in it, crying out together, To Him
Who is seated on the throne and to the Lamb be ascribed the
blessi0ng and the honor and the majesty (glory, splendor) and
the power (might and dominion) forever and ever (through
the eternities of the eternities)! [Dan. 7:13, 14.] [14]Then the
four living creatures (ones, beings) said, Amen (so be it)! And
the elders [of the heavenly Sanhedrin] prostrated themselves
and worshiped Him Who lives forever and ever."*

The book of revelation depicts and explains to us what is goings
to happen when the world is coming to an end. How the antichrist
will proclaim himself as the messiah – *"anti-Christ"*. He is going to
appear and manifest, deceive people to bear his mark (666) which
is the mark of the Beast and send them to hell to their eternal
destruction.

(REV 13:11-18)

*"Then I saw another beast rising up out of the land [itself];
he has two horns like a lamb, and he spoke (roared) like
a dragon. [12]He exerts all the power and right of control
of the former beast in his presence, and causes the earth
and those who dwell upon it to exalt and deify the first
beast, who's deadly wound was healed, and to worship
him. [13]He performs great signs (startling miracles), even
making fire fall from the sky to the earth in men's sight,
[14]And because of the signs (miracles) which he is allowed
to perform in the presence of the [first] beast, he deceives
those who inhabit the earth, commanding them to exact
a statue (an image) in the likeness of the beast who was
wounded by the [small] sword and still lived. [Deut. 13:1-
5.] [15]And he is permitted [also] to impart the breath of
life into the beast's image, so that the statue of the beast
could actually talk and cause to be put to death those who*

*would not bow down and worship the image of the beast.
[Dan. 3:5.] ¹⁶Also he compels all [alike] both small and
great, both the rich and the poor, both free and slave, to
be marked with an inscription [stamped] on their right
hands or on their foreheads, ¹⁷So that no one will have
power to buy or sell unless he bears the stamp (mark,
inscription), [that is] the name of the beast or the number
of his name. ¹⁸Here is [room for] discernment [a call for the
wisdom of interpretation]. Let anyone who has intelligence
(penetration and insight enough) calculate the number of
the beast, for it is a human number [the number of a
certain man]; his number is 666."*

Brothers and Sisters, getting more understanding of what the
Holy Spirit is revealing to me through his inspirations, insight and
foresight about the book of *revelation* the lord explained and revealed
to me a hidden prophecy or a deep revelation about television
(technology) which the lord said is the most powerful technology
in the world and without television there is no way this particular
revelation He is explaining to me was going to come to pass.

And now that the revelation or the prophecy of television has
come to pass or have been fulfilled then that means the time is
right to allow His word to perform on the day that television was
discovered or inverted.

Precious One, do you know or have any idea that television
that we see or watch in our houses and various homes was
discovered through the prophetic word of the lord that was found
in the Bible through the book of revelation.

Believers, little did I know that television is the most powerful
technology in the world based on the word of the lord you might
ask yourself that why am I saying this and this is because in the last
book of the Bible which is *revelation* chapter number eleven verse
number one to fourteen,

(REV. 11:1-14)

Beloved, thank you for taking your time to read this book
because of its powerful *revelation* through the inspiration of the

Holy Spirit now may the lord help me to break the above scripture that you have just read to you for you to understand why am saying television is found through the *revelation* in the bible?

My fellow brothers and sisters, readings the above scripture, it talks about the two witnesses whom God will send to come to the earth getting to this end times to come and prophecy for 1,260 days.

But the most powerful insight that blew my mind with this; is that based on the description of what and how the Bible is describing them, the lord made me under stood that the two witnesses are Prophet Elijah and Prophet Moses whom the lord is going to send to come back to the earth again for an assignment.

Because the scripture declares that *"these men have power to shut up the sky so that it will not rain during the time they are prophesying and they have the power to turn the waters into blood and to strike the earth with every kind of plague often as they want"*. But Precious One, in the Bible from the Old Testament it was only Prophet Elijah that Prophesied for it not to rain for few years.

(1 KINGS 17:1-6).

> *ELIJAH THE Tishbite, of the temporary residents of Gilead, said to Ahab, As the Lord, the God of Israel, lives, before Whom I stand, there shall not be dew or rain these years but according to My word. And the word of the Lord came to him, saying, Go from here and turn east and hide yourself by the brook Cherith east of the Jordan. You shall drink of the brook, and I have commanded the ravens to feed you there. So he did according to the word of the Lord; he went and dwelt by the brook Cherith, east of the Jordan. And the ravens brought him bread and flesh in the morning and bread and flesh in the evening, and he drank of the brook.*

In fact the *revelation* from the Lord are very interesting and powerful and now that we know of Elijah let's see what this description have got to do with Moses. (**EXODUS 7:14-25).**

> *"Then the Lord said to Moses, Pharaoh's heart is hard and stubborn; he refuses to let the people go. Go to Pharaoh in the morning; he will be going out to the water; wait for*

him by the river's brink; and the rod which was turned to a serpent you shall take in your hand. And say to him, The Lord, the God of the Hebrews has sent me to you, saying, Let My people go, that they may serve Me in the wilderness; and behold, heretofore you have not listened. Thus says the Lord, In this you shall know, recognize, and understand that I am the Lord: behold, I will smite with the rod in my hand the waters in the Nile River, and they shall be turned to blood. The fish in the river shall die, the river shall become foul smelling, and the Egyptians shall loathe to drink from it. And the Lord said to Moses. Say to Aaron, Take your rod and stretch out your hand over the waters of Egypt, over their streams, rivers, pools, and ponds of water, that they may become blood; and there shall be blood throughout all the land of Egypt, in containers both of wood and of stone. Moses and Aaron did as the Lord commanded; [Aaron] lifted up the rod and smote the waters in the river in the sight of Pharaoh and his servants; and all the waters in the river were turned to blood. And the fish in the river died; and the river became foul smelling, and the Egyptians could not drink its water, and there was blood throughout all the land of Egypt. But the magicians of Egypt did the same by their enchantments and secret arts; and Pharaoh's heart was made hard and obstinate; and he did not listen to Moses and Aaron, just as the Lord had said. And Pharaoh turned and went into his house; neither did he take even this to heart. And all the Egyptians dug round about the river for water to drink, for they could not drink the water of the Nile. Seven days passed after the Lord had smitten the river."

People of God continuing with the deep revelation of the lord we now know that it was only Prophet Moses that the lord send him to Egypt to threatened king Pharaoh with plague as often as ten and out of it he changed their water into blood.

Believers this is very deep and I hope you are enjoying the sweet revelation of the lord. Also the scripture from the book of revelation continue to declare that after these two witnesses have finished with their testimony, the beast that comes up from the

Abyss will attack them and overpower and kill them. Their bodies will lie in the street of the great city, which is figuratively called *Sodom* and *Egypt* for three and a half days men from every people, tribe, language and nation will "**gaze**" on their bodies and refuse them burial.

In fact this is very deep but interesting, now people of God the Bible declares that every people, every tribe, every language and nation will **gaze** on their bodies which is the bodies of Prophet Elijah and Moses.

But I asked myself this question, how possible can the people in the whole wide world at the same time gather in or around to **gaze** (*another word for* **gaze** *is watch, see or look*) the bodies of this two prophets.

Precious one, please be in my shoes and let's try to figure out this together, I believe this is impossible. But the Holy Spirit answered my question with a question that "*when an important football or soccer match, champions league or world cup is being played, do everybody in the world goes to watch the ball or game live at the stadium or where it is being played*"? I answered in my spirit that no!

And the Holy Spirit asked me again, then where do people who are not able to go and see the soccer match being played at the stadium watch the game? And sharply I answered "*by the help of television or through the help of television*".

Suddenly I bow my heard and stopped writing to worship the lord, could you just believe that without the help of television there is no way possible this prophetic revelation of Prophet Elijah and Moses world have come to pass?

But by the innovation of television every people, tribe, language and nation can **gaze**, watch, see or look at their bodies from all over the world without traveling to *Sodom* and *Egypt* to **gaze** their bodies.

In fact the lord is wonderful and I thank Him for opening and revealing hidden revelation and Prophecies in the bible to me, am blessed and I urge everyone reading this book to love, believe in the lord and accept His son JESUS CHRIST as your lord and master savior for the prophecies which has just been revealed to you through this book speaks to us clear that JESUS CHRIST is the son of God and He is going to be here on earth again to take His chosen ones with Him to Heaven so please let everyone who has or haven't repent from his or her sins and those who don't believe, in God should do so at this very moment for JESUS CHRIST can come any moment from now.

My fellow friends am saying you should believe in God and accept His son JESUS CHRIST as your lord and master savior because Jesus Christ stands for repentance and it was for this reason that He allowed Himself to be sacrificed as the Holy lamp of God for His Holy blood to be used to wipe our sins.

Supposing repentances is not important or not necessary then why would Jesus Christ allow Himself to be used as a sacrificed, be disgraced, bitterly beaten and crucified to death nakedly on the cross? Precious one this is because repentance is very much needed for each and every Single soul that exists on this earth for God loved us so much that He doesn't want us his children to suffer eternal destruction after the second coming of His son Jesus Christ.

(JOHN 3:16).

> *For God so greatly loved and dearly prized the world that He [even] gave up His only begotten (unique) Son, so that whoever believes in (trusts in, clings to, relies on) Him shall not perish (come to destruction, be lost) but have eternal (everlasting) life.*

People of God, repentance is what Jesus Christ came to preach to us before He was crucified because is very important for each and every single soul that exist on this planet to repent or gain repentance because death and eternal destruction is the penalty for those that refuses to repent.

CHAPTER THREE

END TIMES

Many people in the world or I will say men, women of God or preachers both prophets, apostles, pastors and bishops are spending their time and their precious days to manipulate, calculate and even estimating the exact hours, minutes and seconds of the day Jesus Christ the son of our living God will be appearing again.

But I declare to the world that the end times is not about calculating and manipulating or people trying to define the exact hours, minutes or seconds our lord and master savior is coming again but the question is; are we ready and prepared for his coming or have we complete, accomplish and fulfill the assignment and task he entrusted to us; as his children.

Don't we have any port holes or question marks in our lives to fill or to be answered? Because on many chapters and verses in the bible that has declare to us that no one knows or no one will know the exact day or time Jesus Christ will show himself to us again, but people finds it a joke, some are making mockery of it and others are making money of it.

Even Jesus Christ himself admitted that he don't know the day or time he will be appearing again to us but he gave us a clue and he interpreted the signs that we will see when the end time is getting near or when the world is coming to an end. And *"Jesus went out, and departed from the temple: and his disciples came to him for to show him the buildings of the temple.*

2 And Jesus said unto them, See ye not all these things? verily I say unto you, There shall not be left here one stone upon another, that shall not be thrown down.

3 And as he sat upon the Mount of Olives, the disciples came unto him privately, saying; tell us, when shall these things be? And what shall be the sign of thy coming, and of the end of the world?

4 And Jesus answered and said unto them, Take heed that no man deceive you.

5 For many shall come in my name, saying, I am Christ; and shall deceive many.

6 And ye shall hear of wars and rumours of wars: see that ye be not troubled: for all these things must come to pass, but the end is not yet.

7 For nation shall rise against nation, and kingdom against kingdom: and there shall be famines, and pestilences, and earthquakes, in divers places.

8 All these are the beginning of sorrows.

9 Then shall they deliver you up to be afflicted, and shall kill you: and ye shall be hated of all nations for my name's sake.

10 And then shall many be offended, and shall betray one another, and shall hate one another.

11 And many false prophets shall rise, and shall deceive many.

12 And because iniquity shall abound, the love of many shall wax cold.

13 But he that shall endure unto the end, the same shall be saved.

¹⁴ And this gospel of the kingdom shall be preached in all the world for a witness unto all nations; and then shall the end come.

¹⁵ When ye therefore shall see the abomination of desolation, spoken of by Daniel the prophet, stand in the holy place, (whoso readeth, let him understand :)

¹⁶ Then let them which be in Judaea flee into the mountains:

¹⁷ Let him which is on the housetop not come down to take anything out of his house:

¹⁸ Neither let him which is in the field return back to take his clothes.

¹⁹ And woe unto them that are with child, and to them that give suck in those days!

²⁰ But pray ye that your flight is not in the winter, neither on the Sabbath day:

²¹ For then shall be great tribulation, such as was not since the beginning of the world to this time, no, nor ever shall be.

²² And except those days should be shortened, there should no flesh be saved: but for the elect's sake those days shall be shortened.

²³ Then if any man shall say unto you, Lo, here is Christ, or there; believe it not.

²⁴ For there shall arise false Christ, and false prophets, and shall shew great signs and wonders; insomuch that, if it were possible, they shall deceive the very elect.

²⁵ Behold, I have told you before.

²⁶ Wherefore if they shall say unto you, Behold, he is in the desert; go not forth: behold, he is in the secret chambers; believe it not.

²⁷ For as the lightning cometh out of the east, and shineth even unto the west; so shall also the coming of the Son of man be.

²⁸ For wheresoever the carcase is, there will the eagles be gathered together.

²⁹ Immediately after the tribulation of those days shall the sun be darkened, and the moon shall not give her light, and the stars shall fall from heaven, and the powers of the heavens shall be shaken:

³⁰ And then shall appear the sign of the Son of man in heaven: and then shall all the tribes of the earth mourn, and they shall see the Son of man coming in the clouds of heaven with power and great glory.

³¹ And he shall send his angels with a great sound of a trumpet, and they shall gather together his elect from the four winds, from one end of heaven to the other.

³² Now learn a parable of the fig tree; When his branch is yet tender, and putteth forth leaves, ye know that summer is nigh:

³³ So likewise ye, when ye shall see all these things, know that it is near, even at the doors.

³⁴ Verily I say unto you, This generation shall not pass, till all these things be fulfilled.

³⁵ Heaven and earth shall pass away, but my words shall not pass away.

(Matthew 24:1-50)

Precious one, the end time is not a joke but something which is about to happen reality and I believe with the above scripture we can even confirm that some of the signs that will take place before Jesus Christ appear has already or is still happening in our world today.

Jesus Christ took his precious time to discuss and analyzed the end times to his disciples and followers because they were curious and wondering to know the exact time and day all this will happen; where, when and how it will happen. But Jesus Christ being so good, kind and merciful took his time to explain the evil days ahead of mankind to us. He declared about the wars that will come upon nations and kingdoms, sexual immoralities that will come upon mankind, children rising against their parents and the anti- Christ coming in the absence of the *messiah* also will be proclaiming himself as the *messiah*.

Therefore why can't we just ignore the question that we can never get the answer and focused on the things that is paving the way or arousing the attitude of mankind to go against God or making the atmosphere conducive for the anti-Christ to come in to operate or perform?

Many people nations, tribe's languages think the greatest and ever powerful tool the devil (SATAN) uses or is using to convert people, children of God to his kingdom in this end times is lust, sexual immoralities, drunkenness – I mean worldly pleasures.

Yes I believe so these are some factors he uses but I want to draw your attention to this tool as well as a strategy which may have or might not come across your thought. Now think about this, we all believe the Devil (SATAN, DECIEVER, and SEDUCER) was a mighty Angel created by God.

And as the Angel of the Highest God, a celestial being became corrupted and was thrown to the earth by arch angel Michael because he was not strong and powerful enough.

> *"Then war broke out in heaven. Michael and his angels fought against the dragon, and the dragon and his angels fought back. ⁸ But he was not strong enough, and they lost their place in heaven. ⁹ The great dragon was hurled down—that ancient serpent called the devil, or Satan, who leads the whole world astray. He was hurled to the earth and his angels with him"*

(Revelations 12:7-9).

Now think about this, for celestial being to become corrupted whilst in heaven there is no sin even the environment of heaven does not allow anyone to sin. Angels were not made of dust (body) they have no flesh they were made of spirit and fire. By reading the bible and making researched we understand that Lucifer was corrupted with *pride*.

The bible makes it clear that Lucifer was a mighty angle of God an angel of light, who was gifted with voice very powerful in singing, worshiping and praising God; he was a leader of a group of Angels who sing to praise and worship God. The Devil was a chorister (a choir leader). Highly anointed with the gift of voice, therefore he realized that, "*he can sing to move God and heaven*" but why all the praise and worship is going to God, and "*I Lucifer who is doing the singing i am not acknowledged*".

And because of his powerful, sweet and lovely voice he was able to deceive and seduce some angels to embark him war against God. But my problem is why or how come the devil realized that even as a celestial being whom wasn't created to know good and evil; he have been corrupted and overtaken by *pride* and now he is thrown onto earth then why shouldn't he used this as a strategy to corrupt Gods children.

Therefore I want you to realize something revealed to me by God, the beginning and the end, Alpha and Omega, the first and last the creator of heaven and earth and the creation of Lucifer himself; God is very aware of the ways and means of the Devil, his strategic ways and tools he uses to corrupt, deceive seduce and convert God's children to his kingdom (HELL).

Because of this when God who is the visible form of Jesus Christ came through humbleness and came as a humble person. He humbled himself to be born in a manger (sheep's house), humbled himself to the things of this world, portrayed he is nothing yet He is the owner of this world and the entire things in it both good and bad.

Just imagine the one who created heaven and earth because of him everything came into existence without Him no one would have been found on this planet. Think of this Jesus would have come or appear from the richest part of the earth, He would have chosen to be born in a castle so that he will be from a royal family.

But even the owner of the universe decides to humble himself for God, he was conceived in disgrace; born in disgrace, the woman who anointed his feet and prepare him for burial was a prostitute and Jesus Christ died nakedly on the cross which was in a disgrace too.

The greatest secret behind this powerful revelation is that Jesus Christ rejected pride and took hold of humbleness and never felt proud of himself from the they he was born till the day he died on the cross.

Precious people have we wonder why God have to allow his only begotten son to go through a process of disgrace in all of his lifetime on earth. I believe this is a very big question we need to be pondering over and over again till we get the insight and foresight to the answer.

Then why would you human being consider yourself so high above all things, you look down on others because of your riches or success? Because you were born at a very beautiful place and you have the ability to travel all over the world without limitations, your parents are rich for you to get through better education but some people didn't have the opportunity so you see yourself to be on top of everything but by the revelation in this book I declare to you that - *all is pride that have taken over your life therefore I urge you to regret and repent, let God knows that you are nothing before him, all is by his grace and mercies and by the Holy spirit.*

May I used this opportunity to break this evil attitude which is leading people astray and sending many nations, tribes and languages to their eternal destruction.

Why I am saying *pride* is the powerful tool of the devil he uses to steal God's children, example is a person who is deeply drunk; he or she feels on top of everything.

Precious one when you have this abusive spirit of *pride* in you, you don't fear God. You might think you fear God because you go to church and even sings in the church but Satan was even a singer in heaven yet was corrupted with *pride* how much more you being a singer on earth.

This tool is what Satan uses to steal and has used to steal and draw many souls to him (Satan).

Even in the world today people go to church yet have chains or anklets on their legs. People go to church yet wear or bear tattoos on their skin (body), but to be honest with you tattoo are even dangerous and represent the mark of the beast.

I need you to take your time to read the revelation I am about to reveal to you concerning *tattoo*.

Are you aware that the only thing that separates the spiritual world is Heaven and Hell? Now the Bible declares that;

"So a man thinks in his heart is as he is"

(Proverbs 3:27)

Now we all believe that whatever happens in the realm of the Physical has already took place in the spiritual world. Because it's the spiritual world that controls the physical world.

And we should be aware that when you die your soul or spirit lives in the spiritual world or rest in the spiritual world.

And when you die your spirit or soul still function with the elements or senses of life (humanities). That's your senses to feel, touch, hear, see, and smell. If you disagree lets depend on the story from the bible;

(Luke 16:19-26)

"There was a rich man who dressed in purple and fine linen and lived in luxury every day. At his gate was laid a beggar named Lazarus, covered with sores and longing to eat what fell from the rich man's table. Even the dogs came and licked his sores.

The time came when the beggar died and the angels carried him to Abraham's side. The rich man also died and was buried. In hell, where he was torment, he looked up and saw Abraham far away, with Lazarus by his side. So he called to him, Father Abraham, have pity on me and send Lazarus to dip the tip of his finger in water and cool my tongue, because I am in agony in this fire.

But Abraham replied, son remember that in your lifetime you received your good things, while Lazarus bad things but now he is comforted here and you are in agony. And besides all this, between us and you a great chasm has been fixed, so that those who want to go from here to you cannot, nor can anyone cross over from there to us"

From the above scripture simply testify what exactly am trying to explain; So I ask you, if you have **TATTOO** on your body physically which means your spirit or Soul have received it in the realms of the spirits. That's why it have manifest physically on your body.

Now tell me the truth which place or where in the spiritual would do you think you can get or receive **TATTOO**.

Because there are only two places you can think of in the spiritual world. HEAVEN & HELL

Therefore I believe that you know in your spirit that HEAVEN will and can never provide you with tattoo. Therefore where do you think you will receive it from in the spiritual world before it manifest in the realms of the Physical? I believe HELL will be the answer.

Please i am not judging you but breaking this revelation down for you to analyze; after that you can judge yourself.

Because I don't think God will allow you to place a tattoo on his Temple (BODY) because our body is the temple of God and a temple of prayer.

> *"Do you not know that your body is a temple of the Holy Spirit, who is in you, whom you have received from God? You are not your own; 20 you were bought at a price. Therefore honor God with your body,"*

(1 Cor. 6:19-20).

So don't you think for your Spirit or Soul should go to Hell to take TATTOO the devil has marked you as his slave because you bear his mark.

Which is the mark of eternal destruction? Tattoo is also six (6) letter words. And six (6) in the bible represent that mark of the BEAST (666). Six (6) is an evil number.

Please don't be deceived by the world for the devil is very tricky. Because of *pride* you have a tattoo or because you want to show off - people are taking tattoos.

I know people get TATTOO out of love – "little did you know that some love comes with PRIDE".

The fact that you love someone doesn't mean you should wear their names and Logos on your body for your body is the temple of God and must be kept pure and holy.

You claim you love someone by destroying the temple of God or disobey the rules and commandments of God what sense does it make.

"For obedience is better than sacrifice and for the disobedience is the spirit of divination".

We also don't fight against Flesh and blood but rather Spirit of darkness, principalities.

Do you think God blessed us so we can have the capabilities to disobey His Commandments?

The fact that God has blessed you doesn't mean you are greater and higher than his blessings and commandments then you begin to disrespect your foundation where God picked you from. May God have mercy and pity for your soul or spirit to reposition and restructure you?

For God opposes the proud and give grace to the humble. Because the devil (Lucifer) Pride himself – he thought he was greater and higher in heaven but God repositioned him from Heaven to hell.

So I ask you, if you are proud or filled with pride on earth. Do you think God will reposition you from **EARTH TO HEAVEN** – or from **EARTH TO HELL**?

Children of God I believe it is time we regret and repent from so many things the devil has stolen us and its killing us to perform. *"For he came to steal, kill and destroy"*

(John 10:10)

Now if you are wearing or accepting different types of tattoo's on your skin don't you think that is a symbol of Satanism and I believe it all comes with pride and I don't think anyone in this world who is born of a woman and fears God will take, bears or design his or her skin with different types of tattoo's.

This even gives me the revelation that in the end times those who will bear or accept the mark of the beast (666) on their skin (body) will be the ones who are filled with pride. Because the devil is a symbol of pride and it is pride that is detestable to God.

With this revelation I think we shouldn't harden our heart or still be dump. Because in the end times the mark of the beast will be tattooed on the skin of those who will choose to worship the beast Therefore tell me that tattoo has nothing to do with *the mark of the beast – 666.*

Why am I saying the devil is the symbol of pride? I want you to remember with me from the beginning of the bible after God's creation. The bible declares that it was the old serpent (snake) that came to deceive Eve in the Garden of Eden to break the loyalty between God and mankind by convincing them to eat the fruit God have warn them not to eat.

Apparently, why is the bible using serpent to represent Satan and literally we all know that serpent is a snake. This tells me the characteristic of a snake is pride therefore if you are with pride or you are proud of yourself in this world then you are exactly like the snake (serpent).

Coming to think of it, the skin of a snake (serpent) bears or is design with different types of tattoos. Besides the true nature of a snake is very nasty and most of everyone in this world knows that snakes or all types of snakes are not good animals. That's why God cursed it and made mankind despise it from the beginning of creation. So the Lord God said to the serpent, "Because you have done this,

"Cursed are you above all livestock and all wild animals! You will crawl on your belly and you will eat dust all the days of your life.

15 And I will put enmity between you and the woman, and between your offspring[a] and hers; he will crush[b] your head, and you will strike his heel."

(Genesis 3:14-15)

Therefore people of God enjoying this revelation, tattoo come with pride and pride comes with the devil whose true nature and character symbolizes that of a snake, (old serpent and dragon).

The revelation in this book is beyond my thought and no one can be able to write a book of revelation of this kind unless it is authorized from God and the direction of the Holy Spirit.

In fact this book made me went through a period of heavenly thinking, because when God told me to write this book and the revelation begun, I found it very difficult to sleep and think normally at times because it was beyond my brains (mind).

I sometimes felt on ease with the pen because the anointing was too powerful for the revelation I was having. Therefore is my prayer that before and after reading this book the anointing and impartation of heavenly wisdom and knowledge should be drop in your system and open your minds, also edifies your spirits soul and heart.

Again, I pray that before and after reading this book the Holy Spirit should come upon you and the power of God also over shadow you.

People of God the end time is already here in the world because everything around us speaks of the hungriness of the end times; especially like I said earlier in the previous chapter that technology is what is going to end the world. Why will I be saying this over and over again because technology is avoiding Christians to pray fervently during these days. Because many Christians have their much focus on their phones or their tablets and spend more time on the internet than with Jesus Christ.

Technology is paving the way for the anti-Christ to come into the world to perform and distribute his product *"the mark of the beast – 666"*.

The reason am saying this is I want us all to be aware of how cell phones are being upgraded day in day out, the devil is using the functions of cell phones and its upgrading's social apps or the social networks on the internet to win the Christian market. Why am I even saying this because many Christians does not even carry bible with them to church in this days because everything is now designed on their Mobile phones. People of God why do you think the devil is ignoring the original bible now, because of the Holy Spirit that stays with the bible always. The Holy Spirit will never stay or can never stay with your mobile phones because at the same time you have worldly music's and worldly entertainment on them.

Please I am urging us to be wise and seek the wisdom of God to let us know what is coming into the world.

Precious one could you believe that before the innovation of cell phones many people were having good marriages and healthy relationships but in the world today cell phones and its social networks are distracting many healthy and well-built marriages. Now just imagine because of common cell phones - people are stealing to have it, because of cell phones people are committing adultery and even fornicating to have it and because of this same cell phones we are being led astray of indecency communications and transfers of uncensored videos and pictures which are detrimental to our spiritual and Christian life.

For instance a Christian or a believer can be on a social network to chat with their friends or make unnecessary gossips whilst they can use that time to meditate on the things of God or read the bible.

Please I believe we are all aware of what I am talking about because there are many social networks in the world today and it has brought or bring distraction and indecency attitude between God and mankind this is because many Christians or people of God spend a lot of their time on these social networks and before they realized they have not even prayed for the day or spend quality time with God all in the name of the innovation of cell phones and its social apps and functions.

My fellow Christians I want you to be aware of this and quickly repent from this attitude because the devil is using technology and expensive ones of course, beautiful and fascinating phones to steal children of God in the world today.

Why should a believer who's supposed to spend time with God and meditate on the things of the Holy Spirit but because of these social networks many believers and Christians have backslide also break their precious relationship with God based on their cell phone and it social functions that buys all their time and they even refuse to do their quite time and devotions.

Now precious people why do you think cellphones is now an object of attraction in the world. Everybody is trying to get cell phone or everyone in the world is having a mobile phone.

If we could take notice; our banking system is now being generated on the cellphones that you don't even need to go to the bank or carry money on you but you can buy some thing or order something and if you have a cellphone you can pay for your stuff there and then.

People of God the system of carry money on us is about to be over because money affairs is now being designed on our cellphones and so called technology – therefore we shouldn't be surprise when our chips and microchips in our cellphones become the currency to be spent in the world.

Children of God we need to wake up and be spiritually wise so we can ignore the devil with his end time innovations.

People of God, I want you to take your time and understand what I am talking about. If you could draw your attention to this; before when you take a picture with your cell phone or when you upload your pictures on this social networks it doesn't ask you when and where you took the pictures but in the world today when you take a picture with your cell phone or upload your pictures on this social networks it ask you when and where you took the pictures.

And people of God have you sit down or by any chance ask yourself why the cellphone or the social networks is asking you when and where you took the pictures. What did they need this information for, of what purpose or of what benefit will it be to them if they should know when and where you took your pictures.

Precious one I think it is time we need to be wise and calculate all this tricky innovations because these are all contribution of the end times or these are all paving the way for the world to come to an end also for the easy access of the *anti – Christ* to come in to operate and share his mark - 666.

Because if your location is on the cellphone or on the social networks it makes or it is going to makes it very easier for the *anti-Christ* to find or locate you.

Also Precious one the bible declares that we should be wise and calculate *this mark of the beast – 666.*

But little do we know that the mark of the beast cannot be calculated because is a fixed figure or a total sum of an amount of money.

The bible didn't give us any multiplications, subtractions, additions or divisions for us to use it to calculate this amount of money – six hundred and sixty six (666).

In that sense why don't we be conscious or be wise about the things that prevent us from getting closer to God and stop debating over an amount of money or a fixed figure of numbers that cannot be subtracted or divided.

People of God I want us to look around us in the world today, what is preventing us from getting close to God? What is defiling our children, what is stealing us, killing us and destroying our relationship with our father in heaven?

For me I will say *technology* is doing most of the destruction why am I saying this? Because of technology many of us don't respect the power or powers of God anymore; technology is making it impossible for people to believe in the greatness of God.

For instance with the GPX, tom-tom or the car locator – you can just enter your address or zip code and the car will take you to your destination. How interesting people of God, the world is becoming very fascinating by technology which is blinding us from seeing or perceiving that the world is coming to an end.

In fact these are the things I believe we should spend time accessing and calculating because we must be wise of these innovations and inventions. I know very well that many people have spent time and some are still spending time to calculate or figure out *the mark of the beast which is – 666* (six hundred and sixty six).

But my dear friends how or why do you spend time trying to calculate an amount or a figure that is fixed whilst it doesn't have any fractions, equations or square roots beside it?

From my point of view based on these revelation inspired by the Holy Spirit what I will say is; the amount or figure we are trying to calculate is a mark in other words is a symbol that represent something; so is a symbol that represent the beast – *anti Christ*.

But if you should say this mark or symbol 666 in words is six hundred and sixty six then it sound like an amount of money (currency) but we don't know whether it is in US dollars, Great Britain pounds or Euros.

People of God I deeply believe in my heart that many people, nations, tribes and different types of languages are trying so hard to calculate or figure out this mark of the beast – 666.

But if I were you people of God I will rather advice myself with this revelation and be right with God because that is the number one thing mankind should do or focus on.

Because the kingdom of God or the end time is not a matter of calculating, estimating or trying to figure out numbers, time, hours, minutes and seconds to know when Jesus Christ will come or where, when and how the *anti-Christ* will appear.

We should stop miscalculating and rather focus on how to be able to enjoy eternal life and one thing we all need to know and understand is the bible tells us that Jesus Christ will come or appear again the same way he went to heaven that means if anyone is to come on earth saying he is the messiah but didn't appear from heaven as Jesus Christ will come back or appear again is a liar or a false Christ.

But this is a matter of us preparing and making ready for Jesus Christ as his soldiers so when he appears he is going to take us with him. We should make sure and try to fulfill and accomplish the assignment he has given us.

Many people don't even know the assignment Jesus Christ has entrusted to us yet instead of preachers to preach to the ignorant people about how the kingdom of God will be like or what the kingdom of God is about they rather prophesy to make money, preach Gods favor to be rich and successful, preach about tithes and consecrated seeds and donations that can buy them luxurious cars and build them outrageous mansions.

This was exactly what Nicodamus was doing "he was a preacher, an elder and theological expert in the synagogue – the bible declares that he was very rich and a professional teacher of the law, but with these revelation inspired by the holy spirit what I realized about *nicodamus* is; he search for knowledge, wisdom and theological revelation about the law to use on people and I believe he makes money out of them.

Because the bible described this man as a rich and a very wealthy person but based on his story in the bible it never elaborate on how he became rich or the type of business he was doing and how he became wealthy.

All we know from the bible is he was rich but yet still he try found out the knowledge and wisdom about the preaching of Jesus Christ. So the bible declared that he followed Jesus Christ around and one night he came to Jesus and asked him questions about where he got or learned his teachings from or how did he gain that powerful knowledge and wisdom to teach the gospel like that.

But Jesus Christ replied him - *"Nicodamus the kingdom of God is not about seeking after knowledge, indulging in good deeds or worldly gains but the kingdom of God is about faith - to believe in God and his only begotten son Jesus Christ.*

People of God I honestly want us to believe and accept that the kingdom of God is about *faith*; and faith is ability and ability is hard work and hard work is strength and strength is endurance. This is the people that will enter the kingdom of God those who will *endure* to the end.

At this point I will depend on a scripture for us to know the truth of what am talking about concerning the kingdom of God. The bible declared in .....

> *Again, it will be like a man going on a journey, who called his servants and entrusted his wealth to them. [15] To one he gave five bags of gold, to another two bags, and to another one bag,[a] each according to his ability. Then he went on his journey. [16] The man who had received five bags of gold went at once and put his money to work and gained five bags more. [17] So also, the one with two bags of gold gained*

two more. ¹⁸ *But the man who had received one bag went off, dug a hole in the ground and hid his master's money.*

¹⁹ *"After a long time the master of those servants returned and settled accounts with them.* ²⁰ *The man who had received five bags of gold brought the other five. 'Master,' he said, 'you entrusted me with five bags of gold. See, I have gained five more.'*

²¹ *"His master replied, 'well done, good and faithful servant! You have been faithful with a few things; I will put you in charge of many things. Come and share your master's happiness!'*

²² *"The man with two bags of gold also came. 'Master,' he said, 'you entrusted me with two bags of gold; see, I have gained two more.'*

²³ *"His master replied, 'Well done, good and faithful servant! You have been faithful with a few things; I will put you in charge of many things. Come and share your master's happiness!'*

²⁴ *"Then the man who had received one bag of gold came. 'Master,' he said, 'I knew that you are a hard man, harvesting where you have not sown and gathering where you have not scattered seed.* ²⁵ *So I was afraid and went out and hid your gold in the ground. See, here is what belongs to you.'*

²⁶ *"His master replied, 'You wicked, lazy servant! So you knew that I harvest where I have not sown and gather where I have not scattered seed?* ²⁷ *Well then, you should have put my money on deposit with the bankers, so that when I returned I would have received it back with interest.*

²⁸ *"'So take the bag of gold from him and give it to the one who has ten bags.* ²⁹ *For whoever has will be given more, and they will have abundance. Whoever does not have, even what they have will be taken from them.* ³⁰ *And throw that worthless servant outside, into the darkness, where there will be weeping and gnashing of teeth.'*

(Matthew 25:14-30)

Now precious one I believe we have understand it properly from the above scriptures that the kingdom of God is about God giving us talent and talent means gift or money - am saying talent means gift or money because during the days of king Solomon; talent is what is used (measure) as the name of their money or currency. *"The weight of Gold that Solomon received yearly was 666 talents"*

(1 kings 10:14)

And the gift of God to his children is for us to use it to fulfill or accomplish an assignment. Therefore he has giving us this gift according to our ability that means if you have faith you are able to accomplish more if not you accomplish less and if you don't even accomplish nothing you will be burnt in hell.

Precious one I want you to tap into your thought and understand the revelation very well, the more your ability the more your faith; because faith is something that you hope for and because you hope for it you keep on working very hard until you achieve your success.

And for us to enter the kingdom of God is for us to be able to fulfill or accomplish the assignment God has given us. Because in life if you don't have a purpose at your destination or where you are going you will or can never get there, we have a purpose here in this world that is why we are here therefore we must accomplish and fulfill our task for us to be able to enter the kingdom of God.

In fact I really thank God and the power of his holy spirit for such a deep revelation he is revealing to me to write this book.

People of God this not by my might or by my power but this powerful revelation is beyond my thought, knowledge and my wisdom. But this is directly giving to me by God through the inspiration of the Holy Spirit because what are in this book are strong dreams, obvious visions and prophetic hearing from the lord. The only thing that involves my strength was for me to be obedient and listen to put them on paper and publish it as a book to send these powerful words of God across the world.

With this one I know it might be important to some people but to others it might sound abnormal but whom am I not to do as the Lord wish. Writing this book has not been easy for me because of its strong and direct prophesies and just from the beginning of this chapter *end times*.

Precious people of God I can't end this chapter by not sharing what the lord wants me to share with you, the *prophetic visions* the lord showed me concerning the *end times*.

- For the lord showed me in a prophetic vision that strong wars will break out even what we have seen or witness already is just the beginning of birth pains because there is a time coming when different nations will join together to strike other nations.

There will be a great confusion in the United States of America because of its disobedience and blasphemy for its law to allow *female husbands and male wives* also the legalization of gay marriage.

> *"Woe to the shepherds who are destroying and scattering the sheep of my pasture! Declares the Lord. Therefore this is what the God of Israel, says to the shepherds who will tend my people: Because you have scattered my flock and driven them away and have not bestowed care on them, I will bestow punishment on you for the evil you have done, declares the Lord. I myself will gather the remnant of my flock out of all the countries where I have driven them and will bring them back to their pasture, where they will be fruitful and increase in number. I will place shepherds over them who will tend them and they will no longer be afraid or terrified, nor will any be missing, declares the Lord.*

(Jeremiah 23:1-4)

Now please my fellow brothers and sisters, why are we pretending as if everything is okay about this allowing *female husbands and male wives also gay marriage*.

This is the doing of Lucifer who is trying to tarnishing the image of God because *"God created us in his own image"*. Therefore how can the image of God indulge in such an abominable act? Even from the beginning of the bible when man (Adam) needed a companion, God did not give him the same Adam (man) but rather gave him Eve (female). Therefore it should be male for a female or a female for male. Why are we behaving and acting lesser than animals this is a total blasphemy and a typical abomination that causes desolation.

Even animals don't live or act like how human beings are acting; have you heard or seen a male dog flirting or sexing a male dog or any type of male or female animal sexing it same kind, please I believe the answer will be no!

Now in most of the countries like united states of America or United Kingdom; dogs or any other pets are not even allow to fornicate or have sex with some ones dog or pets of the same kind when the owner is aware, then why are we treating human beings like that of low value and as degrading species.

This is an insult to God and his creation, the government value animals more than human beings in some civilized countries. Why are we then happy about a country that value the ethics of animals but disregard the values of mankind?

Why or how can God bless a country that insults and blasphemes his name, image and creation in fact this is terrible, we should wake up and seek the mercies of God?

-Therefore because of this there will be an outbreak of incurable diseases, illness and sickness in America and other parts of the world that has legalized gay marriage and these will let many children of America run out of it but God said to me that he will be using this to select or drag his chosen ones out of the belly of this nation – United States of America.

This is the strong reason why *Medicare* are now being planted in people before you can be hospitalized at the hospital, many people think is not mandatory but later it will be because the *microchip Medicare* is meant for the future but not today and if you don't have it implanted in you; you can never be received at the hospital and this is another abomination that causes desolation because why do Christians need *microchip Medicare* implanted in them whilst we are healed by the blood of Jesus Christ. This *Medicare* is totally from the devil because it is trying to let people ignore, forget and reject the power of Jesus Christ in his blood. The devil is trying to let the Blood of Jesus Christ that brought salvation into the world be meaningless to his people.

But many nations will hate the abominable rules and government of United States of America and many countries will join together to fight against United States of America but will never succeed.

In a prophetic vision I saw a very big conference hall that bears the flags of **London, ECOWAS** and **Israel** – and I know London is the head of all European nations strictly I will say on top of the world because the currency is powerful than every currency in the world and we all know money is power, also **London** is the center that operates or I will say controls United Kingdom; and **ECOWAS** is all African nations joined together – which is going to one day happen I believe it has already begun with *biometric passport* and *e-zwich banking system*; and with **Israel** I will say is a country of its own because no matter what the world will try to harm Israel, that is a country or a place God will always protect and his covenant will not depart from them and Israelites are Jews and as we all know and the bible declares that – *Salvation is from the Jews.*

Therefore there is going to be a time that many people, nations, tribes and languages will run to seek refuge in these mentioned nations.

But the lord said to me that these nations will be the entrance of the *anti-Christ* because they will join together for the uprising of the *anti – Christ* who will call himself the messiah – *the God of Mercy* and this God of mercy will have something to do with women and little children.

"And the lord lifted my spirit to a place called *London Boulevard* where I saw a man's face on a screen dress like a Jew and his name was *The God of Mercy*".

People of God I need you to break this down with me concerning the three nations I mentioned earlier, they are all six alphabets join together.

LONDON – 6
ECOWAS – 6
ISREAL - 6

Please does the calculation mean anything to you because this exactly represent *the mark of the beast* which the bible talks about in (Revelation 13:18)

> *this calls for wisdom "if anyone has insight let him calculate the number of the beast for it is man's number. His number is 666.*

But people of God with the above calculation we realized that they are countries, cities or nations that has come together to represent the mark of this beast.

with my insight, I strongly believe that there is a time coming that countries, cities, states and nations are going to join together to use or spend one currency since the mark of the beast is going to be used to buy or sell.

Precious people let's take our time to understand whatever am trying to explain to you, is my prayers that the holy spirit himself inspire and motivate your intelligence to clearly get the insight of what is going on in this *end times.*

In the book of ***Revelation 13:13-18.***

> *"And he doeth great wonders, so that he maketh fire come down from heaven on the earth in the sight of men,*
>
> *[14] And deceiveth them that dwell on the earth by the means of those miracles which he had power to do in the sight of the beast; saying to them that dwell on the earth, that they should make an image to the beast, which had the wound by a sword, and did live.*
>
> *[15] And he had power to give life unto the image of the beast, that the image of the beast should both speak, and*

cause that as many as would not worship the image of the beast should be killed.

[16] And he causeth all, both small and great, rich and poor, free and bond, to receive a mark in their right hand, or in their foreheads:

[17] And that no man might buy or sell, save he that had the mark, or the name of the beast, or the number of his name.

[18] Here is wisdom. Let him that hath understanding count the number of the beast: for it is the number of a man; and his number is Six hundred threescore and six.

Believers the bible declares that anyone who does not bears *the mark of the beast-666* could not be able to buy or sell. That means the mark of the beast will be used or spend as a currency to trade in the whole wide world.

My brothers and sisters I would love you to picture this insight with me – the bible is saying that the number 666 is the mark of the beast but do we know that the dragon is powerful than the beast and do we also realized that in the above scriptures it is the dragon that gave the authority to the beast.

"Men worshipped the dragon because he had given the authority to the beast and the also worshipped the beast and asked who is like the beast? Who can make war against him?"

Therefore precious one in the bible the devil, Lucifer, old serpent or Satan is described as the **Dragon.**

"The great dragon was hurled down – that ancient serpent called the devil or Satan, who leads the whole world astray. He was hurled to the earth and his angels".

(Revelations 12:9)

These means the dragon who gave the beast authority over every tribe, people, language and nation is **S**atan. Now I want us to calculate this from the bible it says that the beast is a man because his mark is a man's number - 666.

"This calls for wisdom – if anyone has insight let him calculate the number of the beast, for it is man's number. His number is 666".

Precious one this means the beast is a man a normal human being born of a woman and already in the world as the *anti-Christ* but I suggest his authority has not been given to him yet but I believe very soon his authority will be given to him or it is in the process.

I know many people in the world believe that it is Satan that will be born in to the world in the form of man as the *anti-Christ* but the bible has just made us understand that the dragon who is Satan is the one going to give authority to the beast and the beast will oppressed mankind with his mark – 666.

But many people are spending time calculating this mark of the beast because the bible used the world calculate but do we know that there are other words that defines the word calculate. Therefore for the bible to use the word calculate is a spiritual word that means spiritual insight but it doesn't mean that we should try and work the mark of the beast-666 like that of multiplication, addition, subtraction or division.

Still going through the scripture of revelation 13 verse 15 I had the insight that even everyone will be forced to receive the mark on his right hand or on his forehead so that no one could or can buy, sell or trade unless he all she had received the *mark of the beast – 666*.

And the bible declares that this will not just be a mark of the beast but the usefulness of the mark will be use like a currency (money) which will be used to buy, sell or trade. But people of God in this world it is only money or currency that is used to buy or sell something, I hope by now we are getting the picture because *the mark of the beast - 666* will be a currency that is going to be used in the whole wide world. But with this currency we are not going to have it like real money in cash or saved in banks or in our bank accounts but rather going to be designed or *tattooed* on our foreheads or on our right hands.

So anywhere you go you can carry this mark with you before you can do anything in this world whether you want to travel, go to school, hospital, buy food, get a job, buy a car or a house I mean anything you can think of in these world that involves money.

And I believe this will be the time that mankind will be forced to receive the mark of the beast because how are you going to survive the difficult times without food, clothes and shelter.

Children of God this is a very great insight and I believe the Holy Spirit himself is talking to you about this revelation of the *end times* because is going to be real and how troubled mankind is going to be.

In fact we are going to be in a very great distress if we don't repent to be able to escape from this disaster.

This is the very reason the bible declares that we should be watchful or vigilant and pray so that this days does not fall on you like the pregnant woman or on the Sabbath or this day does not come in winter time.

> *"How dreadful lit will be in those days for pregnant women and nursing mothers! Pray that your flight will not take place in winter or on the Sabbath. For then there will be great distress, unequaled from the beginning of the world until now – and never to be equaled again."*

(Matthew 24:19-21)

People of God why is the bible using a pregnant woman, Sabbath day or winter season to explain this times? Precious one what is the condition or what are the conditions of a pregnant woman? Because if we have taken notice of a pregnant woman or women they feel so dull, not active, they are lazy and they feel unwilling to do anything. They can't even run away from the house when there is a fire out break; so you just imagine if you are in this condition spiritually or physically and the tribulation of the end times fall on you. I believe you will be forced to receive the mark of the beast based on your situation spiritually or physical because you can't even endure the persecutions of the beast.

So as on the Sabbath day we are taught not to do any hard work and even on winter times you feel not to go anywhere because it's very cold outside and everyone wants to stay indoors. Going to church even gets very hard, so tell me; why you won't receive the mark of the beast if you can't go to work, can't go to church to seek for Jesus Christ.

In this this times you are spiritually weak and you don't even have the desire to love Jesus Christ know God or fear him how can you then get the desire to endure to the end.

In fact this is not just a joke but is going to be very hard and a bad time for those who will be left behind to experience this *end times*.

Therefore my brothers and sisters I urge you to turn to God, regret and repent from your sins and accept his only begotten son Jesus Christ as your lord and master savior so that you can escape from this disaster.

THE MUSIC INDUSTRY – ENTERTAINMENT

People of God why do you think there is too much money in the entertainment industry especially sports and worldly music because I have been asking God about this for a very long time that; why can he bless people who don't even spend much of their time acknowledging him and not even promoting the things of his kingdom and his son Jesus Christ.

But recently God gave me an answer that *"He has never blessed and can never bless anyone in this world more than his word"*. Then why are this worldly entertainers or I will say superstars, celebrities and musicians having so much money which is not coming from God.

Now the answer is; God drew my attention to the ancient days, how the romans entertain themselves by throwing humans to creatures like the lions or beasts in their entertainment stage or place called the **ARENA**. This arena are like stadiums of today, how people circle around to enjoy what is being performed and others gambling all over. God said to me that *this is what generated what we are seeing or experiencing today* because is the ROMAN EMPEROR who throws huge amount of money into world sports, worldly music's and all worldly entertainment.

Besides why do you think they will involve such amount of huge and great money into things like that, this is to desensitize those involve and those with talent?

Because if there is too much money in entertainment people will lose control of their talent and the devil will buy their talents, gifts and time from them in the exchange of luxurious life and also withhold them from focusing on the truth, reading the Bible, spending their time with God, thinking that it is God blessing them but it come from Satan?

Precious people we need to be wise and focus because the devil is smart enough to desensitize us with worldly gains and buy our salvation with money.

God showed me from the bible about his coming concerning this worldly music and entertainment which is now winning the Christian market.

> *"In a flash, in the twinkling of an eye, at the last trumpet.*
> *For the trumpet will sound, the dead will be raised imperishable, and we will be changed".*

(1 Corinthians 15:52)

The bible declared that before the coming of Jesus Christ there is going to be sound of a trumpet blown by an angel and if anyone who hears this sound will be raptured.

Precious one I believe sound from a trumpet is music and music is also a form entertainment. Therefore why do you think the devil is promoting worldly music's and all sort of evil entertainment of today? Because he knew very well about this spiritual sound the angel of the lord will make from his trumpet.

And if the devil is able to promote more music's in the world and pleasurable entertainment people's spiritual attention and focus will be lost and stolen and our ear drums will be block by worldly entertainment which will let many of Jesus Christ chosen one's be left behind.

People of God we need to be very wise and make sure our souls and spirits are being activated by the spiritual things of God so that we can be raptured when his spiritual trumpet is blown, for there is only two type of music God likes *praises* and *worship* songs and he uses Preaching of the gospel to entertain himself. Therefore anything apart from this is purely evil.

-I was attacked by a prophetic word from God which is for Kenye Omari West who is popularly known as Kenye West all over the world. This happened on the date of 16.08.2013 in the evening between the hour of 7pm to 8pm which was on the Friday at a Prophetic conference which I attended but wasn't the one who hosted the program or the one to preach.

The program begun by singing and worshipping the lord whilst I was praying through the worship suddenly the drummer who was playing the drum took the microphone from the lady leading the worship and he begun to sing more of deep worship songs which moved the atmosphere and I believed everyone was moved in the spirit and many of us were praying in the spirit.

But the lord opened my eyes and I saw the face of Kenye west on the front of the white t-shirt that the drummer who is now leading us through the worship had on, and I asked myself, why is this guy wearing a t-shirt that have the face of Kenye West printed in front? Because a Christian should have nothing to do with people who disrespect God and make mockery of his son Jesus Christ in their songs, Kenye West has been using the name of God and His Son Jesus Christ in most of his songs and they play this Songs in the club whilst the people will be drinking alcohol, smoking and prostitutes stripping and others prostituting also all sought of indecent acts.

But God spoke to me and asked me; *do I know why Kenye West is with us in this conference today? I answered, no!* And God said to me that it is because *"he is my servant a prophet"*. Oh my gracious! God this is not just hard for me to believe and accept but how can this be and who in the world is even going to believe this because everybody who hears this will think am totally insane and not just insane but I was born lunatic. Oh! Jesus Christ help me with this one, this is what I shouted in my spirit. Humbly and by the obedience of the Holy Spirit I felt weak to allow myself to receive this prophetic word from God which I begun to think and this was like magic.

God begun to talk speedily to me within a few minutes by saying; have I noticed this rapper, I said not really then He started, this rapper has been making worldly songs that bears my name and my son's Jesus Christ. Also in his videos has been making mockery of my kingdom by using satanic symbols to portray myself and the host in heaven apparently this worldly songs that he makes is being played at clubs whilst people having been drinking alcohol, prostituting and all sought of satanic acts but he is supposed to be *"my servant a prophet"* to win souls for me and promote my kingdom business instead he has allowed himself been stolen by the devil (Satan) with worldly anxieties such as fame, wealth and luxury which will fade away within a twinkle of an eye but my *"word"* will remain forever.

Listen to me carefully, do you remember from the bible what I did to Saul Paul who later became Paul, how he make mockery of my word, my children (Christians) my kingdom by running around to persecute those that believed in me. I turned his heart of negativity to positivity on his way to Damascus to kill torture and persecute my children I spoke to him and by the time he got to Damascus it wasn't killing anymore but rather promoting the kingdom business.

(Acts 9:1-31)

Meanwhile, Saul was still breathing out murderous threats against the Lord's disciples. He went to the high priest ²and asked him for letters to the synagogues in Damascus, so that if he found any there who belonged to the Way, whether men or women, he might take them as prisoners to Jerusalem. ³As he neared Damascus on his journey, suddenly a light from heaven flashed around him. ⁴He fell to the ground and heard a voice say to him, "Saul, Saul, why do you persecute me?"

⁵ "Who are you, Lord?" Saul asked.

"I am Jesus, whom you are persecuting," he replied. ⁶ "Now get up and go into the city, and you will be told what you must do."

⁷ The men traveling with Saul stood there speechless; they heard the sound but did not see anyone. ⁸ Saul got up from the ground, but when he opened his eyes he could see nothing. So they led him by the hand into Damascus. ⁹ For three days he was blind, and did not eat or drink anything.

¹⁰ In Damascus there was a disciple named Ananias. The Lord called to him in a vision, "Ananias!"

"Yes, Lord," he answered.

¹¹ The Lord told him, "Go to the house of Judas on Straight Street and ask for a man from Tarsus named Saul, for he is praying. ¹² In a vision he has seen a man named Ananias come and place his hands on him to restore his sight."

¹³ "Lord," Ananias answered, "I have heard many reports about this man and all the harm he has done to your holy people in Jerusalem. ¹⁴ And he has come here with authority from the chief priests to arrest all who call on your name."

¹⁵ But the Lord said to Ananias, "Go! This man is my chosen instrument to proclaim my name to the Gentiles and their kings and to the people of Israel. ¹⁶ I will show him how much he must suffer for my name."

¹⁷ Then Ananias went to the house and entered it. Placing his hands on Saul, he said, "Brother Saul, the Lord— Jesus, who appeared to you on the road as you were coming here—has sent me so that you may see again and be filled with the Holy Spirit." ¹⁸ Immediately, something like scales fell from Saul's eyes, and he could see again. He got up and was baptized, ¹⁹ and after taking some food, he regained his strength.

Saul in Damascus and Jerusalem

Saul spent several days with the disciples in Damascus.
20 At once he began to preach in the synagogues that Jesus is the Son of God. 21 All those who heard him were astonished and asked, "Isn't he the man who raised havoc in Jerusalem among those who call on this name? And hasn't he come here to take them as prisoners to the chief priests?" 22 Yet Saul grew more and more powerful and baffled the Jews living in Damascus by proving that Jesus is the Messiah.

23 After many days had gone by, there was a conspiracy among the Jews to kill him, 24 but Saul learned of their plan. Day and night they kept close watch on the city gates in order to kill him. 25 But his followers took him by night and lowered him in a basket through an opening in the wall.

26 When he came to Jerusalem, he tried to join the disciples, but they were all afraid of him, not believing that he really was a disciple. 27 But Barnabas took him and brought him to the apostles. He told them how Saul on his journey had seen the Lord and that the Lord had spoken to him, and how in Damascus he had preached fearlessly in the name of Jesus. 28 So Saul stayed with them and moved about freely in Jerusalem, speaking boldly in the name of the Lord. 29 He talked and debated with the Hellenistic Jews,[a] but they tried to kill him. 30 When the Believers learned of this, they took him down to Caesarea and sent him off to Tarsus.

31 Then the church throughout Judea, Galilee and Samaria enjoyed a time of peace and was strengthened. Living in the fear of the Lord and encouraged by the Holy Spirit, it increased in numbers.

This is a exactly what I will do to this rapper Kenye West if he doesn't turn back to me in his right mind but continue to use the name above all names, the name bigger and stronger than his entire generation both before and after; *I will also never stop to make mockery of him which I have even started.* Because the heart of the king is in my hands and I turned and Channel it to where I pleases.

> *"The heart of the king is like rivers of water in the hand of the Lord. He turns it where He wishes."*

- Proverbs 21:1.

Listen, I God is going to make sure this rapper bears the cost of how he makes people think and understands me, my son Jesus Christ and my Kingdom. In this end time I am going to use him to change many rappers who are mine but the devil has use worldly gains and pleasures to steal them from me and about to kill and send them into their eternal destruction.

I am God the one who gave them their eyes to see, nose to smell, ears to hear, voice to be heard, mouth to talk and all the senses of humanities. If they believe there is anyone before and after me they should try this, by parking up their riches, wealth, properties and luxuries to go and dwell in their own universe. Upon all that they think they have got they should go and create or buy their own planet to dwell in and then I God cannot be God over them.

> Behold I am coming soon - <u>11</u>*"Let the one who does wrong, still do wrong; and the one who is filthy, still be filthy; and let the one who is righteous, still practice righteousness; and the one who is holy, still keep himself holy."* <u>12</u>*"Behold, I am coming quickly, and My reward is with Me, to render to every man according to what he has done.* <u>13</u>*"I am the Alpha and the Omega, the first and the last, the beginning and the end."*...
>
> (Revelation 22:11-13).

This is overwhelming people of God and a direct strong prophecy but whom am I not to do the will and wish of God but I pray that may the transporter of the holy spirit transport this prophetic to the entire world and to the one who needs to hear, listen and know what says the lord.

CHAPTER FOUR

ATONEMENT

Atonement is the procedure of reconciling sinners to God, I know one will ask that why should a person be reconciled with God? Because of our sins precious one; atonement was a process or I will say a major sacrifice done or perform in the old testament once a year in the most holy place by the high priest to shed blood and make sacrifices of bulls and goats for the forgiveness of persons sins to be granted also clean the sins of humanities.

Let me use this opportunity to hints on the elements involved in atonement.

- Sin of humanity (Isaiah 6:7)
- Blood must be shed (Hebrews 9:19-22)
- Substitutionary sacrifice is offered (1 John 2:2)
- Guilt is transferred to the substitute (2 Corinthians 5:21)
- Forgiveness is granted (Romans 3:23-25)

Atonement is an event or an occasion that symbolizes sacrifices in the Old Testament and this sacrifice was done once a year.

People of God, you know before the birth of Jesus Christ; mankind's sins were not just confessed with our mouths for our forgiveness to be granted but rather have to be a procedure of shedding blood of goats and bulls also offering burnt sacrifices by the high priest before once sins can be forgiven or atone for.

And this was done once a year, so if you sin against God or men during those times you have to wait for that special *Day of Atonement* before you can be clean of your sins.

> *"The Lord spoke to Moses after the death of the two sons of Aaron who died when they approached the Lord.* ^{2} *The Lord said to Moses: "Tell your brother Aaron that he is not to come whenever he chooses into the Most Holy Place behind the curtain in front of the atonement cover on the ark, or else he will die. For I will appear in the cloud over the atonement cover.*
>
> ^{3} *"This is how Aaron is to enter the Most Holy Place: He must first bring a young bull for a sin offering[a] and a ram for a burnt offering.* ^{4} *He is to put on the sacred linen tunic, with linen undergarments next to his body; he is to tie the linen sash around him and put on the linen turban. These are sacred garments; so he must bathe himself with water before he puts them on.* ^{5} *From the Israelite community he is to take two male goats for a sin offering and a ram for a burnt offering.*
>
> ^{6} *"Aaron is to offer the bull for his own sin offering to make atonement for himself and his household.* ^{7} *Then he is to take the two goats and present them before the Lord at the entrance to the tent of meeting.* ^{8} *He is to cast lots for the two goats—one lot for the Lord and the other for the scapegoat.[b]* ^{9} *Aaron shall bring the goat whose lot falls to the Lord and sacrifice it for a sin offering.* ^{10} *But the goat chosen by lot as the scapegoat shall be presented alive before the Lord to be used for making atonement by sending it into the wilderness as a scapegoat.*
>
> ^{11} *"Aaron shall bring the bull for his own sin offering to make atonement for himself and his household, and he is to slaughter the bull for his own sin offering.* ^{12} *He is to*

take a censer full of burning coals from the altar before the Lord and two handfuls of finely ground fragrant incense and take them behind the curtain. ¹³ He is to put the incense on the fire before the Lord, and the smoke of the incense will conceal the atonement cover above the tablets of the covenant law, so that he will not die. ¹⁴ He is to take some of the bull's blood and with his finger sprinkle it on the front of the atonement cover; then he shall sprinkle some of it with his finger seven times before the atonement cover. ¹⁵ "He shall then slaughter the goat for the sin offering for the people and take its blood behind the curtain and do with it as he did with the bull's blood: He shall sprinkle it on the atonement cover and in front of it. ¹⁶ In this way he will make atonement for the Most Holy Place because of the uncleanness and rebellion of the Israelites, whatever their sins have been. He is to do the same for the tent of meeting, which is among them in the midst of their uncleanness. ¹⁷ No one is to be in the tent of meeting from the time Aaron goes in to make atonement in the Most Holy Place until he comes out, having made atonement for himself, his household and the whole community of Israel.

¹⁸ "Then he shall come out to the altar that is before the Lord and make atonement for it. He shall take some of the bull's blood and some of the goat's blood and put it on all the horns of the altar. ¹⁹ He shall sprinkle some of the blood on it with his finger seven times to cleanse it and to consecrate it from the uncleanness of the Israelites.

²⁰ "When Aaron has finished making atonement for the Most Holy Place, the tent of meeting and the altar, he shall bring forward the live goat. ²¹ He is to lay both hands on the head of the live goat and confess over it all the wickedness and rebellion of the Israelites—all their sins— and put them on the goat's head. He shall send the goat away into the wilderness in the care of someone appointed for the task. ²² The goat will carry on itself all their sins to a remote place; and the man shall release it in the wilderness.

23 "Then Aaron is to go into the tent of meeting and take off the linen garments he put on before he entered the Most Holy Place, and he is to leave them there. 24 He shall bathe himself with water in the sanctuary area and put on his regular garments. Then he shall come out and sacrifice the burnt offering for himself and the burnt offering for the people, to make atonement for himself and for the people. 25 He shall also burn the fat of the sin offering on the altar.

26 "The man who releases the goat as a scapegoat must wash his clothes and bathe himself with water; afterward he may come into the camp. 27 The bull and the goat for the sin offerings, whose blood was brought into the Most Holy Place to make atonement, must be taken outside the camp; their hides, flesh and intestines are to be burned up. 28 The man who burns them must wash his clothes and bathe himself with water; afterward he may come into the camp.

29 "This is to be a lasting ordinance for you: On the tenth day of the seventh month you must deny yourselves[c] and not do any work—whether native-born or a foreigner residing among you— 30 because on this day atonement will be made for you, to cleanse you. Then, before the Lord, you will be clean from all your sins. 31 It is a day of Sabbath rest, and you must deny yourselves; it is a lasting ordinance. 32 The priest who is anointed and ordained to succeed his father as high priest is to make atonement. He is to put on the sacred linen garments 33 and make atonement for the Most Holy Place, for the tent of meeting and the altar, and for the priests and all the members of the community.

34 "This is to be a lasting ordinance for you: Atonement is to be made once a year for all the sins of the Israelites."

And it was done, as the Lord commanded Moses.

(Leviticus 16:1-34)

Precious one based on these procedure and performance people were limited to get close to God personally, because it have to be only the high priest who can enter into the tent of meeting at the holy place and with these no one could or can see God one on one.

Too much sins was on the head of the people because imagine a whole year you can ask for forgiveness of your sins once, in fact this was a state of predicament for the people at that time and even loving God and getting into close touches with him was somehow difficult because you can never go to him or call upon him when you are with sin unless the high priest have to do it on your behalf.

But glory is to God that now we can call upon God whether with sin or without sin even goes to him when we sin against him. Because the bible declares that we should be bold and have confidence in us to come to our father in heaven when we sin against him…

> *"For we do not have a high priest who cannot sympathize with our weaknesses, but One who has been tempted in all things as we are, yet without sin. 16therefore let us draw near with confidence to the throne of grace, so that we may receive mercy and find grace to help in time of need."*

(Hebrews 4:16)

People of God this is because of Jesus Christ atoning blood, God have to sacrifice his only begotten son Jesus Christ to atone for our sins; this is because of what and how cleansing of one's sin is complicated to the people in the old testaments or the world, also the limitation of the people getting to know God and who he is, loving him and having a close and personal relationship with him.

Therefore Jesus Christ presented or atoned his blood to God or to the world and through that our sins are forgiven, we are purified from sin, we are freed from sin, we are redeemed, we have peace with God, we are made holy, we are reconciled to other Christians and the power of the devil is destroyed.

God showed me another revelation of why He came on earth in the visible form of His son Jesus Christ. As we all believe he came to take our sin by cleansing us with His blood through crucifixion by dying on thee cross.

But Satan (Lucifer, the Devil) who tries to involve himself with everything God does has made many believers young, adult and old believed that he (Satan) is the opposition of God and has super powers which is never true. Therefore many believers think Jesus Christ on earth was to take also the powers of Satan but I tell you, the devil was given nothing and nothing of him is valuable to Jesus Christ. I say this because Satan is a liar, a thief and a murderer; the bible describes him as "*father of all lies*".

(JOHN 8:44).

You are of your father, the devil, and it is your will to practice the lusts and gratify the desires [which are characteristic] of your father. He was a murderer from the beginning and does not stand in the truth, because there is no truth in him When he speaks a falsehood, he speaks what is natural to him, for he is a liar [himself] and the father of lies and of all that is false.

In this Revelation, God revealed to me by talking to me through the knowledge and wisdom of the Holy Spirit that, if it was because of Lucifer (Satan, Devil) he came on earth he would have remain on his throne and spit (spat) on him (Satan) to make what is crooked – straight.

WHY? Because God said to me, the devil is too inferior for Him and God is too holy to involve himself with the filthy things of Satan.

Therefore God took me through the process of why He has to descend from His holy throne to earth and cleansed us of our sins with His precious blood by dying on the cross.

Yes! We all believe Satan is the founder of sin but the question is, how did he invented it and why are we involved in Satan invention as children of most High GOD.

Through Research and reference from the Bible "it makes it very obvious that the serpent (SATAN) was crafty (SKILLFUL) in deceiving, seducing and lying".

(GENESIS 3:1-24)

NOW THE serpent was more subtle and crafty than any living creature of the field which the Lord God had made. And he [Satan] said to the woman, Can it really be that God has said, You shall not eat from every tree of the garden? [Rev. 12:9-11]. And the woman said to the serpent, We may eat the fruit from the tree of the garden, Except the fruit from the tree which is in the middle of the garden. God has said, you shall not eat of it, neither shall you touch it, lest you die. But the serpent said to the woman, you shall not surely die, [II Cor. 11:2.] For God knows that in the day you eat of it your eyes will b opened and you will be like God, knowing the difference between good and evil and blessing and calamity. And when the woman saw that the tree was good (suitable and pleasant)for food and that it was delightful to look at, and a tree to be desired in order to make one wise, she took of its fruit and ate; and she gave some also to her husband and he ate,. Then the eyes of them both were opened, and they knew that they were naked; and they sewed fig leaves together and made themselves apron like girdles. And they heard the sound of the Lord God walking in the garden in the cool of the day, and Adam and his wife hid themselves from the presence of the Lord God among the trees of the garden.

Firstly, Satan put this invention in the thought of woman (Eve) and ADAM'S (the first man) by seducing and deceived Eve in a very nice thoughts and thinking that if they do what God has commanded and warned them not to do. *'They will die'* but I Satan tells you, you shall not surely die as he said but you will be very wise like God; "So ask yourself EVE - if *He doesn't want you to be wise like HIM why will he tells you to eat all fruits but stay away from this particular fruit and why would He kill you or destroys you after spending his precious and valuable time to create you for the one He love's – ADAM*".

Now we realized that, the devil put the thoughts into woman's (EVE) mind and she also transferred it to man (ADAM) and secondly they **acted** (Action) on their thoughts (idea) and they produced sin. Now after acting or after their action they realized what they have produced. The bible said *they came back to their senses and realized that, they were naked so they covered their private parts and begun to hide in the Garden (EDEN).*

Now I want you to think about this carefully because it has also set me thinking too. Why ADAM and EVE did covered their private parts after their actions (**by eating the fruit**) but before they ate the fruit they were naked yet did not realized it until their actions were done.

Listen believers, the revelation behind this is very deep, God created ADAM (First man) and through man's thought God caused ADAM to sleep very deeply and then formed (created) EVE out of his (ADAM) one ribs. Here I know you are asking yourself and thinking because I said it's through man's thought God created EVE.

Yes! I said this because after God had finished creating man (ADAM) in his own image. He gave dominion to man to take absolutely control of all living and non-living things. So the bible declare, through this dominion (ADAM) the first man gave names to all living and non-living things. But he realized that the living things are two in their kind, a male and female. Though the bible never tells us what happened after he realized it, we know and believed he would be asking himself questions and thinking all day long. *"So at this point we find out by reading, researching and making reference in and from the Holy bible, God came in to cause ADAM to fall into a deep sleep because God realized and knew what man (ADAM) was thinking, and he created woman (EVE) for Adam (man) to be his helper and support".*

Now please listen to this revelation carefully, after Adam (Man) realized God has created something out of what he was thinking then ADAM said *"Now this is bone of my bone, flesh of my flesh"* she shall be called WOMAN.

Meaning of WOMAN - **W**omb of **M**an.

Listen to this carefully, for men who are saying if God knew what woman will do to man yet he created woman, this is the answer. After creation of woman and Adam's confession and appreciation to what God have given him - listen to what God said.

(GENESSIS 2:24 – 25)

> *Therefore a man shall leave his father and his mother and shall become united and cleave to his wife, and they shall become one flesh. And the man and his wife were both naked and were not embarrassed or ashamed in each other's presence.*

For this reason a man will leave his father and mother and be united to his wife and they will become one flesh. Now take note of this the bible continue to say that the man and his wife were both naked and they felt no shame...

(GENESIS 2:25).

> *And the man and his wife were both naked and were not embarrassed or ashamed in each other's presence.*

Here comes your Answer, Please take note of this; Do you know that God, After pronouncing ADAM (man) and EVE (Woman) as couples God never told them how they shall or should bring forth their children (off springs), so this was what God was waiting to see how Adam will go about it; through his (ADAM) dominion or by using his wisdom knowledge, authority and power God has given him.

Now think about this carefully, see how ADAM (Man) choose to bring forth his off springs or how to produce children.

Here, even though God has pronounced Adam (men) and Woman (EVE) as husband and wife he never taught them how to produce their children or bring forth their off spring. But we realized God has given Man dominion on everything and anything, so He (GOD) expect Adam (man) to bring forth without corrupting it because of his (ADAM) wisdom (Dominion) or come to God for guidance and to teach them the way.

But we found out that, the devil, deceiver and seducer came in to seduced, deceived and put thought of negativity unto their mind and they acted (action) on it corruptibly so the seed (sperm) they produced were corrupted because it wasn't the idea of God. That is why the scripture declares *"for we have been born again not of perishable (corrupted) seed (sperm) but of imperishable (incorruptible) through the living and enduring word (Jesus – Blood) of God".*

(1 PETER 1:23)

> *You have been regenerated (born again), not from a mortal origin (seed, sperm), but from one that is immortal by the ever living and lasting Word of God.*

Now you know what Adam (Man) and Eve (Woman) choose instead of choosing the Blood of Jesus. They choose corruption (Sperm) as the way to bring forth their off spring which was not the saying of God. But also we realized that before Adam (Man) gave names to the living and non – living things, all names he gave to them was the exact idea and expectation of God.

(GENESIS 2:19-20)

> *And out of the ground the Lord God formed every [wild] beast and living creature of the field and every bird of the air and brought them to Adam to see what he would call them; and whatever Adam called every living creature, that was its name. And Adam gave names to all the livestock and to the birds of the filed; but for Adam there was not found a helper meet (suitable, adapted, and complementary) for him.*

Therefore I want you to ask yourself, before your mother could give birth to you; she and your father have to go through a process of corruption (sperm). So before you came out you were already corrupted.

Then I believe, God said to himself *"for me not to involve my son in this corruption and filthy actions (sin) generated through man and woman I could use my own blood known as JESUS to cancel,*

Wash and break this corruptible seed (sperm) by using the incorruptible (Blood) seed to cleansed this action (sin) by my sons blood" so who ever believe in him will become born again. *So ask yourself, why the words **born again** and will **not perish** but have **everlasting life**".*

These is why, God have to descend from his throne to earth by his own blood through the visible form of Jesus Christ, to make what has been crooked – straight, negative– positive, Reschedule what has been wrongly schedule to position what has been wrongly position and to make unclean - clean, unrighteous – righteous, ungodly – godly and unholy – holy.

Now the Holy Spirit will answer your questions; Because Jesus Christ could stay away from sin and never sinned because he was not made of sperm (corruptible seed) that's why he is so different from us.

Please I need you to think about this, why should someone who is coming to the world to save you from your sins is not already saved. Therefore Jesus coming on earth must already be saved before he could save us; that' is why the bible said in;

(LUKE 6:41-42)

Why do you look at the speck of saw dust in your brother's eye and pay no attention to the plank in your own eye? How can you say to your brother, Brother let me take the speck out of your eye: when you, yourself fail to see the plank in your own eye? For hypocrite, first take the plank out of your eye and him you will see clearly to remove the speck from your brothers' eye.

Therefore Jesus did not have to appear on earth as we appeared on earth so he could save us with His precious Blood. Jesus was already saved before he came to saved us and must therefore indeed be saved before he can save us.

Brothers and sisters this revelation need a supernatural insight and foresight to understand what the Holy Spirit is trying explain to us therefore I pray for the understanding of the spirit on you to gain the insight and foresight of this revelation.

CHAPTER FIVE

CONFESSION

The first thing to redemption is *confession* but I know someone might ask what redemption is, redemption is the state of being saved from the power of evil (sin). This compound word means "*to depart from and be released to.*" When one repents of his sins, he departs from the enslavement of sin and is released to freedom in Jesus Christ. A typical example is Paul on the road to Damascus; he departed from his enslavement of sin and was released to a new freedom found only in Jesus Christ. He stated it this way in Ephesians "*in him we have redemption through his blood, the forgiveness of sins, according to the riches of his grace.*

Redemption is free but not cheap that which frees you also enslaves you, redemption involves the choice to make Jesus the lord and master of your life therefore you become his slave. No one is free we are all slaves to that which governs and controls our lives.

What I meant when I said redemption involves choice is because God allows us to make our own choices and no one delineates this more clearly than Jesus according to him we can choose:

- A narrow gate or a wide, The big crowd or the small crowd, the narrow road or a wide road (Matthew 7:13-14)
- We can choose to build on rock or sand (Matthew 7:24-27)
- Serve God or riches (Matthew 6:24)
- Be numbered among the sheep or the goats (Matthew 25:32-33)

God even give eternal choices and these choices have eternal consequences *"then they (those who rejected God) will go away to eternal punishment, but the righteous to life"*

(Matthew 25:46).

Have you ever wonder why there were two crosses next to Jesus Christ? Why not six or ten? Have you ever wonder why Jesus was in the center? Why not far left or far right? Could it be that the two crosses on the hill symbolize one of Gods greatest gifts? The gift of choice.

The two criminals have so much in common, Convicted by the same system. Condemned to the same death, surrounded by the same crowd equally close to the same Jesus Christ in fact they begin with the same sarcasm, the two criminals also said cruel things to Jesus Christ (Matthew 27:44) but one Changed.

One of the criminals on the cross begun to shout insults at Jesus Christ *"aren't you the Christ? Then save yourself and save us"* but the other criminal stopped him and said "you should fear God! You are getting the same punishment he is, we are punished justly getting what we deserve for what we did. But this man has done nothing wrong, then he said "Jesus remember me when you come into your kingdom." Jesus said to him, I tell you the truth, today you will be with me in Paradise"

> *"One of the criminals who hung there hurled insults at him: "Aren't you the Messiah? Save yourself and us!"*

> [40] *But the other criminal rebuked him. "Don't you fear God," he said, "since you are under the same sentence?*

⁴¹ We are punished justly, for we are getting what our deeds deserve. But this man has done nothing wrong."

⁴² Then he said, "Jesus, remember me when you come into your kingdom.[a]"

⁴³ Jesus answered him, "Truly I tell you, today you will be with me in paradise."

(Luke 23:39-43)

Precious one I hope you are enjoying the sweet biblical revelation the holy spirit is breaking down; in fact am loving it myself but I want us to use this to know what confession is and what confession does to us and by the power of God through his son Jesus Christ see how just confessing with your mouth you are saved from your sins and redeemed by the blood of Jesus Christ.

With the two criminals one choose to confess that he is a sinner but have now regret and he wants to reconcile with God and trust me he was saved but with the other one instead of confessing his sin and gained salvation he choose to throw insults on the one who can save him and believers he perished.

Please by these I want you to give thanks to God for his son Jesus Christ that he has make redemption so simple through confession of our sins. I will say God is powerful because I need you to think about this; what is powerful, heavier, stronger, bigger and greater than the blood of Jesus Christ and tell me what sin in this world that it can never be clean or cleansed with the blood of Jesus.

Precious one the blood of Jesus Christ is ready for you to confess your sins and it will erase your sins and iniquities just at the open of your mouth to accept that you are a sinner and you want or need Jesus Christ to be the master savior or governor of your life.

The bible declared that he is a honest and Justice God that it doesn't matter how great or strong your sins are or it doesn't matter how you are heavy burdened by your sins, is only the matter of confessing your sins to him believing that you have regret and now you have repent from them.

In addition may I also brief you with another powerful revelation about what am trying to make you understand about confession and I strongly believe that the holy spirit will help you tap into your thought and get the deeper understanding of how is so necessary and very relevant to confess your sins and turn to God if you have not repented.

Didn't the shepherd leave the 99 sheep and pursue the one lost? Didn't the housewife sweep the house until the lost coin was found? Yes, the shepherd did, the house wife did, but the father of the prodigal son, remember, did nothing.

- The sheep was lost innocently.
- The coin was lost irresponsibly.
- But the prodigal son left intentionally.

The father of the prodigal son gave him the choice; Jesus Christ gave both criminals the same. There are times when God sends thunder to stir us. There are times when God sends blessings to lure us. But then there are times when God sends nothing but silence as he honors us with freedom to choose where we spend eternity.

And what an honor it is! In so many areas of life we have no choice. Think about it, you didn't choose your gender, you didn't choose your siblings, and you didn't choose your race or place of birth.

Sometimes our lack of choices angers us. "It is not fair" we say. It's not fair that I was born in poverty or from a poor home or that I sing so poorly or that I run so slowly. But the scales of life were forever tipped on the side of fairness when God planted a tree in the Garden of Eden. All complaints were silenced when Adam and his descendants were given free will, the freedom to make whatever eternal choice we desire. Any injustice in this life is offset by the honor of choosing our destiny in the next.

Wouldn't you agree? Would you have wanted otherwise? Would you have preferred the opposite? You choose everything in this life and God chooses where you spend the next? You choose the size of your nose, the color of your hair and your DNA structure, and God chooses where you spend eternity? Is that what you would prefer?

It would have been nice for God had let us order life like we order meal. I will take good health and high IQ. But it didn't happen, when it came to your life on earth you weren't given a voice or vote but when it comes to life after death you were, this seems like a good deal.

Have we been given any greater privilege than that of choice? Not only does this privilege offset any mistakes. Think about the thief who repented, though we know little about him, we know this; he made some bad mistakes in life. He also chose wrong crowd, the wrong morals, and the wrong behavior. But would you consider his life a waste? Is he spending eternity reaping the fruit of all the bad choices he made? In the end all his bad choices were redeemed by a solitary *confession*.

You have made some bad choices in life, haven't you; you have chosen the wrong friends, maybe the wrong career, even the wrong spouse. You look back over your life and say, "*if only... if only I could make up for those bad choices.*" You can. Only one good choice for eternity offsets a thousand bad ones on earth.

The choice is yours to just confess your sins and be free from evil and reconcile with God or turn to God. Because how could two men see the same Jesus and one choose to confess to him and other choose to mock him. I don't know but they did. And when one confessed, Jesus loved him enough to save him.

People of God, this is a privilege and a very great opportunity mankind on earth can ever had. Just for you to open your mouth and confess to God your horrible and terrible sins and iniquities are cleansed and erased forever and ever.

For the bible even declared that "he is a faithful and honest God that when you confess your sins to him he is going to forgive you and he will not remember it anymore".

The bible also declares that so far as the earth is far away from the heavens so as the lord our God is going to wipe away our sins.

"For as high as the heavens are above the earth, So great is His loving kindness toward those who fear Him. 12As far as the east is from the west, So far has He removed our transgressions from us. 13Just as a father has compassion

on his children, So the LORD has compassion on those
who fear Him....

(Psalm 103:11-13)

This is only when you confess your sins to him. Precious one I urge you to open your mouth at this point to confess your sins the ones you did intentionally and the ones you did unintentionally.

And why I am saying intentional and unintentional sins is because there are certain sins that you were aware of but yet you love to accomplish them, that is why King David said to the lord to forgive him his hidden faults and willful sins.

> "Who can discern his errors? Forgive my hidden faults.
> *Keep your servant also from willful sins and may they not*
> *rule over me"*

(Psalm 19:12-13)

There are sins that you perform consciously but there are some sins you have committed whilst you don't even know they are sins. But by the inspiration of the Holy Spirit I would love to let us know that "sins that are done unconsciously are called *sins* but the ones that are perform consciously are *iniquities* and yet still the blood of Jesus Christ is capable to forgive and erase all types of abominable sins if only you will humble yourselves and confess.

May we read a story from the bible about a prophet called Isaiah (Isaiah 6:1-11)?

> *"In the year that King Uzziah died, I saw the Lord, high*
> *and exalted, seated on a throne; and the train of his robe*
> *filled the temple. 2 Above him were seraphim, each with*
> *six wings: With two wings they covered their faces, with*
> *two they covered their feet, and with two they were flying.*
> *3 And they were calling to one another:*
>
> *"Holy, holy, holy is the Lord Almighty;*
> *the whole earth is full of his glory."*
>
> *4 At the sound of their voices the doorposts and thresholds*
> *shook and the temple was filled with smoke.*

5 "Woe to me!" I cried. "I am ruined! For I am a man of unclean lips, and I live among a people of unclean lips, and my eyes have seen the King, the Lord Almighty."

6 Then one of the seraphim flew to me with a live coal in his hand, which he had taken with tongs from the altar. 7 With it he touched my mouth and said, "See, this has touched your lips; your guilt is taken away and your sin atoned for."

8 Then I heard the voice of the Lord saying, "Whom shall I send? And who will go for us?"

And I said, "Here am I. Send me!"

9 He said, "Go and tell this people:
"'Be ever hearing, but never understanding;
be ever seeing, but never perceiving.'

10 Make the heart of this people calloused;
make their ears dull
and close their eyes.[a]

Otherwise they might see with their eyes,
hear with their ears,
understand with their hearts,
and turn and be healed."

11 Then I said, "For how long, Lord?"

And he answered:

"Until the cities lie ruined
and without inhabitant,
until the houses are left deserted
and the fields ruined and ravaged,

From the above scripture we have fine the truth ourselves that Isaiah was a prophet of God but he confess his conscious sins that is "am a man of unclean lips (conscious) and I live among the people of unclean lips (unconscious) but by the Grace of our merciful lord he was forgiven both his sins and iniquities.

Brothers and sisters I want to encourage you to forget about how God will forgive you because you think you are a powerful or a strong sinner, you might be a murderer, a prostitute, a criminal thief and others but please it doesn't matter; for Jesus Christ have even make a covenant by or with his blood to forgive us our sins.

> *"This is my blood of the covenant, which is poured out for many for the forgiveness of sins"*

(Matthew 26:28)

As we have testify ourselves from the biblical truth I believe at this point you are not afraid to confess your sins or you don't have to allow the negative spirit of fear and doubt intimidate you from confessing your sins to God.

In the bible many great priests, prophets, powerful kings and many followers of Jesus Christ sinned against God but later turned to God and confessed their sins and reconciled with God and their sins and iniquities where forgiven and erased.

Brothers and sisters this is the reason I meant when I said from the beginning of this chapter that the first thing to redemption is confession because it is the only way that can help us see God. Confessing is good for our spirit, soul and body because when we confess we receive God's mercy, we receive God's forgiveness, we are justified, we receive healing and we become purified.

CHAPTER SIX

Holy Spirit – BAPTISM

On one occasion, while he was eating with them, he gave them this command: "*do not leave Jerusalem, but wait for the gift my father promised, which you have heard me speak about. For John baptized with water, but in a few days you will be baptized with the Holy Spirit*".

So when they met together, they asked him "lord, are you at this time going to restore the kingdom to Israel?"

> He said to them "*it is not for you to know the times or dates the father has set by his own authority but you will receive power when the Holy spirit comes on you and you will be my witnesses in Jerusalem and in all Judea and Samaria and to the ends of the earth.*"

(Acts 1:4-8)

Wonderful! After all that Jesus Christ has done for us on the cross of Calvary he didn't end it there but yet promised us his richest and greatest gift that will empower us to be able to be his witnesses and overpower the devil till the ends of the earth.

Have you wonder why we need this gift in us or be baptized with this gift or why is it so important for Jesus Christ to grant us this gift. And if this gift is not important why would Jesus authorize his disciples not to leave Jerusalem or preached the Gospel until they have been baptized with the Holy Spirit. And if you should realized in the above scriptures it is when you receive the Holy Spirit or when he comes on you then you will be able to witness or preach the gospel to the ends of the earth.

I will say the Holy Spirit signifies Jesus Christ authority, ownership and responsibility for whatever bore his mark in other words I will say the Holy Spirit is *The Mark of Jesus Christ*.

God's imparted Holy Spirit signifies his ownership of us, his authority over us and his responsibility for us, please if you still haven't receive this gift he is still waiting for you.

One of the reasons I love the gift of the Holy Spirit and recommend it to new converts is because it gets us started on the right foot. And it's the most significant gift amongst all the gifts of God. Looking at the great prophets and preachers in the bible that encounter the gift of the Holy Spirit their preaching and teachings were unique and magnificent very powerful and chaos prevailed because the power of the holy spirit also bring confusion in the mind and heart of the enemy (Satan).

> When John the Baptize arrived on the scene of Judea, chaos prevailed. The Holy Spirit moved as john preached in the hearts and lives of those who received his words by faith, order ensued.

> (Mark 1:4-11)

> When Paul arrived in Ephesus, chaos prevailed, Apollo's confused converts were caught somewhere between faith and law, the Holy Spirit moved as Paul preached, convinced and baptized, those converts experienced the holy spirit moving in their hearts and seeing their lives in order.

> (Acts 19:1-7)

Even from the beginning of creation nothing would have been possible or creation would have been impossible without the movement and performance of the Holy Spirit. Why am I saying this?

(Genesis 1:1-5)

Firstly, God created. Everything he created was perfect and good, just as he himself is perfect and good. A perfect and good God can do no less' otherwise, He would be neither perfect nor good, now how is it that the perfectly good creation of a perfect good God came to be "without form, and void? How did darkness come to cover the face of the deep? Are we missing something? Is there some gap between verses one and two of our text? These are some sorts of questions that keep me wondering and are there even answers to such questions?

Despite the revelation and deep inspirations from the Holy Spirit he remains a mysteriously unfathomable God.

The implication here is that nothing was happening and nothing would have happened until the spirit of God moved" Jesus said *"without me, ye can do nothing"*

(John 15:5)

It's enlightening to look at the nothing passages in the Gospels. Jesus once confessed, *"The son can do nothing of himself"*

(John 5:19)

Jesus later promised that with faith as small as a mustard seed *"nothing shall be impossible unto you"*

(Matthew 17:20)

There is quite a lot in these *"nothing"* text but in conjunction with the Holy Spirit moving and performing, God spoke and order ensued, the lights came on and everything begun falling into places.

One thing I ask my self is even God needed the involvement of the Holy Spirit to begin creation then why don't we also need the Holy Spirit in us or on us to begin everything particularly preaching of the Gospel.

All this gives us the powerful reason to pray to God for His gift of the Holy Spirit because it gives you the power to fulfill and accomplish anything and everything, it also makes what seems impossible possible to them that have the gift of the Holy spirit. And this gives me the revelation that anyone who doesn't have this gift is spiritually blind and spiritually poor.

This will be furthered explained by a familiar story about a heroic figure called Naaman. Naaman is afflicted with leprosy and is appalled when he is told that in order to effect his cleansing, all he needs to do is dip himself in the Jordan River, and he refuses to do until he is chided by his servant, *"if the prophet had told you to do something great, wouldn't you have done it?*

Many of us would like to do something great to serve God, we dream of missionary, crusades to the deepest and most remote parts of the jungle. We fantasize about preaching to stadia full of people who hang on our every word. We did like to be Christian philanthropist who is able to fund worthy causes out of our abundance. But how can we accomplish all this great things when we are spiritually blind and poor and refuse to take directions of the Holy Spirit.

Naaman was influential in bringing victory to his king, he was one who was greatly admired and highly sought after yet there was one sad circumstance in his life – he had leprosy.

This is unbelievable, isn't it, that fame, success and prestige don't prevent tragedy and illness from our lives. Think of famous people you can name who have cancer, family strife or tragedy that hits their homes.

Naaman had access to the finest of medical care; but alas there was no cure for his leprosy.

The most significant part of this story is the one who shows the most spiritual discernment is a servant girl in his household. An Israelite, she knew of a prophet in Samaria who could cleanse Naaman if only he could see him. Precious one how many times does God use the weak to shame the strong, the foolish to shame the wise?

Imagine if no one had the gift of the Holy Spirit in Naaman's household how would he have receive his healing. Because Naaman was spiritually poor but physically rich, spiritually blind but physically can see well.

Therefore have we seen why it is so important to receive or gain the gift of the Holy Spirit?

As one with political connections, Naaman attempts to go through channels to set up a meeting with Elisha. He has his king draft a letter to Elisha, when Elisha's king receives the letter he thinks Naaman's king is trying to pick a fight with him and asks" *why does he send someone to me to be cured of his leprosy?*"

Isn't this spiritual blindness that Elisha's king – and the king of God's covenant people – doesn't have enough sensitivity and spiritual discernment to know that there is a man of God full of the holy spirit in their midst?

Elisha heard of the king's request and said" *have the man come to me and he will know that there is a prophet in Israel*"

Precious one do people in your church community, family and friends know that there is the gift of the Holy Spirit in you or on you, do you help people who are lost of the gospel be found, the broken hearted be restored by your gift of the holy spirit and do you give spiritual directions to those that are drifted away from the truth. Do your friends and family know that when they come to you or listen to you they will meet God and be changed?

Naaman goes to see Elisha and is underwhelmed. He deals with one of Elisha's servants rather than Elisha himself. Elisha wanted to communicate that the healing doesn't come from him but came from God. Elisha's mode of cleansing is to have Naaman dip seven times in the Jordan River.

Precious one have you wonder why Elisha wanted Naaman to dip himself in the river before he will be healed, because Naaman wasn't baptized and in his case he must be baptized before God can save him. Please isn't this powerful and the prove and the truthfulness of what am saying.

At first Naaman is out raged. *"If dipping me in a river would cleanse leprosy there are far superior rivers in Syria"* Naaman basically thought. Then his servant asked a question so powerful that it rings through the ages *"if the prophet had told you to do something great, wouldn't you have done it.*

Many of us would be willing to do something great in order to be right with God but what God really wants is *simple trust* and *obedience.*

What great thing brought Naaman's to his healing? His obedience. What great thing brings us salvation? Simple trust in the crucified resurrected and ascended of Jesus Christ.

I believe this powerful story have touched your heart enough to know that the holy spirit is much needed in our lives to be able to accomplish the mission God has set before us. The Holy Spirit is a perfect Gift from God is free but not cheap therefore if you will pray to God for this gift he will give it to you without limit.

This reminds me of how the devil is impersonating this gift on people to deceive them as if they have the Holy Spirit on them but little do they know that is faked. This truly scares me, because many are performing and moving as if their gift is from God but not and this is mind blowing also deceiving even the right sons and daughters of God.

The devil is standing strong on the gift God will pour on his people to deceive many, as the devil know that during the last days God will pour his spirit on many to perform his work the devil is duplicating many of God gift to deceive and draw souls to himself. "'

> *In the last days, God says,*
> *I will pour out my Spirit on all people.*
>
> *Your sons and daughters will prophesy,*
> *your young men will see visions,*
> *your old men will dream dreams.*
>
> *18 Even on my servants, both men and women,*
> *I will pour out my Spirit in those days,*
> *and they will prophesy.*

19 I will show wonders in the heavens above
and signs on the earth below,
blood and fire and billows of smoke.

20 The sun will be turned to darkness
and the moon to blood
before the coming of the great and glorious day of the
Lord.

21 And everyone who calls
on the name of the Lord will be saved.'[a]

(Acts 2:17-21)

Why would a perfect God with a perfect gift that depicts the truthfulness of God should allow the devil perform or act as if he too has the same perfect gift. This draws my attention to the biblical verse that during the last days the devil will intrude in the gifts and operations of God. But how will we the true sons and daughters of God and followers of Jesus Christ know that this is not the doing of the Holy Spirit but the devil.

Until we are baptized in the Holy Spirit or with the Holy Spirit then the bible assure as of it fruit. This is what is expect of the Holy Spirit that comes from God,

"But *now I am going to him who sent me. None of you asks me, 'Where are you going?' 6 Rather, you are filled with grief because I have said these things. 7 But very truly I tell you, it is for your good that I am going away. Unless I go away, the Advocate will not come to you; but if I go, I will send him to you. 8 When he comes, he will prove the world to be in the wrong about sin and righteousness and judgment: 9 about sin, because people do not believe in me; 10 about righteousness, because I am going to the Father, where you can see me no longer; 11 and about judgment, because the prince of this world now stands condemned.*

12 "I have much more to say to you, more than you can now bear. 13 But when he, the Spirit of truth, comes, he will guide you into all the truth. He will not speak on his own; he will speak only what he hears, and he will tell

you what is yet to come. 14 He will glorify me because it is from me that he will receive what he will make known to you. 15 All that belongs to the Father is mine. That is why I said the Spirit will receive from me what he will make known to you."

The Disciples' Grief Will Turn to Joy

16 Jesus went on to say, "In a little while you will see me no more, and then after a little while you will see me."

(John 16:5-16)

I hope by now we have known the truth from the above scriptures ourselves of what is expected of God's Holy Spirit, the bible declares that when the holy spirit comes – he is going to tell us what is going to happen in the future but not what is going to happen in the past. The spirit is not going to give out people's bank details, phone numbers, marriage secrets, names, time and dates, personal or private secretes of individuals.

For we even know that when Rebekah overheard the future blessings of Esau, she overturned the blessings to her second born Jacob and Esau was cursed instead of the lord's blessings.

So I will ask you, what you think it will happen to you when the devil overheard your future blessings or success. I strongly reveals to you that you will totally become the devils target and he is going to make sure he over turns your blessings by fighting against your opportunities, principles, favors and all your efforts.

Do you know that in the old testaments true prophets and men of God don't strictly speak of individual's future greatness in public unless the prophetic message is for the entire community?

Based on this greatest gift of God the devil has developed a similar device to deceive people, destructing and deceiving people. By telling them is their family, mother, father, sister, brother, cousins, aunties' and wife's bewitching them. Please it is not your mother or father who is destroying or delaying your blessings but it is Satan that is operating through them. That is why Jesus said to peter "Satan get behind me" it doesn't mean peter is Satan but it was Satan rather working through peter.

*"Jesus turned and said to Peter, "Get behind me, Satan!
You are a stumbling block to me; you do not have in mind
the concerns of God, but merely human concerns"*

(Matthew 16:23)

People of God this is why we need the Holy Spirit and be baptized with it to be able to gain his directions, guidance, foresights and insights of his ways so the devil can never trap us or so we can never fall into the temptations of the devil or even if we fall into the temptations of the devil we will be able to over power and overcome the devil and bring him to divine judgment.

As the Holy Spirit has instruct me to give out some chapters and verses from the bible, why is important to be filled with the Holy Spirit and the need of the Holy Spirit Baptism in the life of every believer.

- The holy spirit helps you to walk in God's statutes and keep God's ordinance and obey them (Ezekiel 11:19-20)
- The holy spirit gives you the power to live holy (Matthew 3:11)
- He gives you power to be bold witness for God (Act 1:8)
- He helps you to bear the fruit of the spirit (Galatians 5:22-24)
- He helps you to walk in the spirit (Galatians 5:16)
- He helps you in your prayer life (Romans 8:26)
- The holy spirit leads you in your daily life (Romans 8:14)
- He comfort and abide with us forever (John 14:16-17)
- He counsel and teach all things (John 14:26)
- He is our helper, intercessor, advocate, strengthener and standby (John 14:13-21)
- The Holy spirit gives you power to endure hardships and persecutions (Acts 4:13-21)
- He helps in your prayer to edify and fortify your spirit against ungodliness and error (Jude 1:20)
- He helps in your prayer to alter mysteries before God (1 Corinthians 14:2)

- He helps in your prayer during spiritual warfare (Ephesians 6:18)
- The Holy spirit helps you to operate in spiritual gifting's (1 Corinthians 12:1-9)
- The holy spirit is a spiritual gusher – a release of power for service and earthly ministry (John 7:38)

People of God our God is a perfect and a true God, I believe no one can dispute the fact that the Holy Spirit is relevant in our lives. I will tell you that we all need him so much. But have you also ask yourself that why is it that in this recent times prophets and many men and women of God are not preaching the importance or the benefits of the holy spirit, is it because when they teach or preach the holy spirit and help us to be baptized in the holy spirit; our spiritual mind and eyes will open and we will be able to testify their spirit and know what type of spirit their using to operate whether is from God or not.

It is only the Gift of the Holy Spirit that one can use to testify a different spirit which is not from God.

Precious one these wonderful and perfect gifts from our triune God remain unclaimed under Calvary's tree. If you haven't already received yours, the Holy Spirit is still waiting for you.